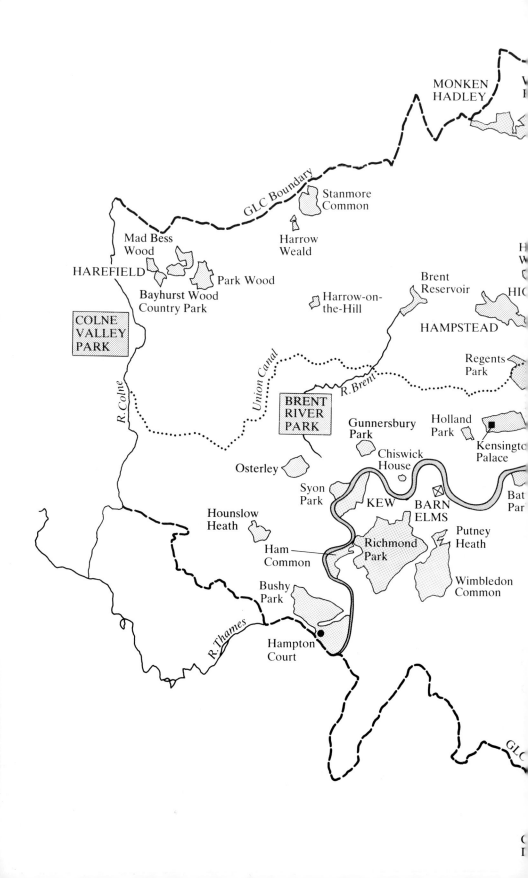

COUNTRY
LONDON

Also by John Talbot White

The Countryman's Guide to the South-East

COUNTRY LONDON

John Talbot White

Illustrated by Oliver Caldecott

Routledge & Kegan Paul

London, Boston, Melbourne and Henley

First published in 1984
by Routledge & Kegan Paul plc
39 Store Street, London WC1E 7DD, England,
9 Park Street, Boston, Mass. 02108, USA,
464 St Kilda Road, Melbourne,
Victoria 3004, Australia, and
Broadway House, Newtown Road,
Henley-on-Thames, Oxon RG9 1EN, England
Set in 10 on 13 Palatino
by Inforum Ltd, Portsmouth
and printed in Great Britain by
the Thetford Press Ltd, Thetford, Norfolk.
Text © the estate of John Talbot White 1984
Illustrations © Oliver Caldecott 1984

Library of Congress Cataloging in Publication Data

White, John Talbot.
Country London.
Bibliography: p.
1. London (England)——Description——1981—   ——Guide-
books. 2. London (England)——Suburbs and environs——Guide-
books. I. Title.
DA679.W53   1984   914.21'204858   83—16013

ISBN 0–7100–9873–1

CONTENTS

Preface   vii

Author's Note   ix

1   The River   1
2   The City   17
3   Royal Parks   33
4   Spas and Commons   47
5   Greenwood   61
6   Downlands   77
7   Epping Forest   91
8   London's Farms   105
9   Waterways   117
10   Deer Country   129
11   Resident Birds   143
12   All that is Green   157

References   167

PREFACE

London is ever changing, its green spaces under constant pressure for new roads, new buildings. The Covent Garden where my father bought and sold country produce at the turn of the century is now a shopping piazza. The rustic view in Kensington Gardens, so admired by Rudolf Steiner and described in the opening of Chapter 3, is now framed by a Henry Moore sculpture. New developments in the Barbican have introduced more greenery by the walls of the old City. Each year the picture will alter, yet the broad canvas painted here remains true. London is one of the greenest of cities: the sights, smells and memories of the countryside past and present await our discovery and enjoyment.

John Talbot White
Greenwich

AUTHOR'S NOTE

Throughout this book, the word 'City' refers to the City of London, whereas 'city' refers to the entire area within the present boundary of the Greater London Council.

I

THE RIVER

One hundred and three swans, cobs, pens and cygnets, paddled slowly round the timbers of a pier along Blackwall Reach. Keeping them company were one Canada goose and three greylag geese taking a winter break from their Baltic homeland. Above them loomed the towers of a sugar refinery. The sloping roofs of the warehouses and the struts of the cranes were lined with feral pigeons, thousands of them. A flock of gulls drifted upstream on the incoming tide, some taking a ride on floating timbers. A ship from Rotterdam cruised slowly by, and as its bow-waves hit the anchored barges they knocked together and the gulls flew off with protesting cries. One pied wagtail stayed on the gunwale, still chirping merrily.

I was looking down at the water creeping up the sloping shore of mud, sand and debris when the blue, metallic flash of a kingfisher broke across the dull morning, an unexpected bonus. I followed the riverside path in the same direction the kingfisher had flown, half hoping for another sighting, and found the anglers gathered by the old Harbour Master's house at Greenwich. They were landing small flatfish with almost monotonous regularity.

Some of the swans had moved down towards Greenwich Pier, looking up with stern eyes in the hope of tit-bits. The anglers were unimpressed but the winter walkers out for Sunday papers and the morning freshener threw bread. Other swans drooped their long necks beneath the water to eat the weeds anchored to the timbers. The mute swans of the Thames are the largest flying birds in London, up to 40 lbs in weight. They are royal birds in fact as well as appearance. Two of the City companies also have ownership rights and, once a year, in summer, the young cygnets are marked at the swan-upping ceremony that takes place upstream beyond the boundaries of London. The bills are nicked, one for the Dyers' Company, two for the Vintners. All the unmarked birds are the birds royal. The swans floated on past the lush green lawns of the Royal Naval College.

When the Tudors built their palace here with its hunting grounds stretching inland to Blackheath, and Henry VIII established the royal dockyard at Deptford, this was a town in London's countryside. The walk to the City led through market gardens and pastures, drainage ditches and windmills. Now it leads through warehouses and housing estates and the Royal Victoria Dock that still keeps a tenuous link with its great past. Alongside the dock entrance is a small garden with a few plane trees and an ancient mulberry knotted with age, protected by a railing, the last relic of one of London's greatest gardens, created by that prince of tree-planters, John Evelyn, whose estate of Sayes Court stood here.

Much of the Evelyn estate and the docks where the Golden Hind was berthed have been transformed into a large housing estate, retaining some of the old rum warehouses and fine eighteenth-century houses in its matrix. The river has been made accessible by a walkway, replete with guns impotently gazing across the river. With a little skilful navigation and a bit of luck, you can follow lanes and alleys from the Pepys Estate (yet another name that perpetuates the great naval tradition of the area) to Surrey Docks. On the way, inscribed stones by the roadsides or built into bridges tell old country stories. One dated 1855 marks the line of the Bermondsey, Rotherhithe and Deptford Turnpike. Another with dates earlier in the century bears the initials of St Paul's, Deptford, and St Mary's, Rotherhithe, the parish boundary that was also the ancient division between the rural counties of Kent and Surrey.

Across the river are the silhouettes of cranes and ship's masts, the granaries and timber warehouses of Millwall Docks on the Isle of Dogs, once in the ancient county of Middlesex. Was it Henry VIII's dogs or the Isle of Ducks? A small riverside garden set up in 1891 on the north bank commands a classic view across to Greenwich. The walls, Millwall, Blackwall, lined with windmills, were the first retaining walls on the riverside. Behind them were the marshes of Stepney and Poplar, with fat sheep and oxen on some of the richest grazing land in the country. Heron, plover and bittern roamed its almost undisturbed solitudes. These were the marshes, the flood plain of the Thames.

The flood plain, more than a mile wide, takes in most of the south bank as far as Southwark. It shows up on the geological map as a yellow band and is of interest to more than geologists. For, all over London, a new map is on display showing the flood plain, the riverside areas most vulnerable to flooding if the Thames rises over its new retaining walls and embankments. From Teddington to Greenwich there are plaques on walls, one, for example, by the seventeenth-century Trinity almshouses at Greenwich, showing previous devastations by the river. January has witnessed some of the worst floods of recent times, 1928, 1953, and 1978 a close-run thing.

The marshes were difficult to build on but easy to excavate for docks. The flood plain became London's dockland starting with London Docks in 1805, Surrey Docks in 1807 and on to Millwall in 1864. Now the docks are losing their trade and becoming deserted basins but even this has its advantage for lovers of wildlife and open spaces. A friend who works in the Royal Albert Docks keeps me posted regularly about his resident cormorant that roosts on a raft of timber, and flies over to join him on the crane. There are eels and dabs and trout in the dock and the cormorant is a dexterous fisher often being mobbed by gulls as it feeds. It takes easy avoiding action by diving. There are herons there, too, enjoying the new freedom of the docks.

As you walk into the dock area from the riverside walk on the Pepys estate, the bridge rises over the outlet of the South Dock and there is a cormorant holding its wings out in heraldic posture, sitting on a raft of rubbish with black-headed gulls, black-backed gulls, mallard and moorhen. This is a posture for drying, for according to some experts the cormorant has a poor waterproofing system. Others say the 'sailing' posture helps digestion. The next bridge leads to the larger basin of the Greenland Dock and the improbable sight of chickens, goats, and other farmyard animals on a patch of waste ground. This farm, which even keeps bees for honey amongst its various activities, started by a group of enthusiasts, may only be a temporary feature of the new landscape, a gallant attempt to bring the countryside back into the heart of the city but any future scheme for the docks ought to leave a space for such a venture as well as to create a wildlife sanctuary, for in the basin itself amongst all the warehouses and quaysides stacked with containers, are upwards of two hundred tufted duck taking advantage of the sheltered water, and a hundred gulls screaming overhead. Closed since 1970, the docks have developed enough natural flora to give cover and food to more than ninety species of birds. Wintering birds can number more than two thousand with pochard, tufted duck, mallard and greater rarities like scaup, red-breasted mergansers and ferruginous duck. As many as forty heron have been sighted at one time.

So successful a bird sanctuary has Surrey Docks become that amongst the breeding species in the summer some entirely new species have been recorded for the first time in recent years so close into the city, such as the lapwing, the ringed plover, the reed bunting, the meadow pipit, the yellow wagtail and the black redstart. And this is in addition to the usual habitués of London's inner city, the sparrows, the starlings, blackbirds, thrushes, pied wagtails and the like. No less than twenty-eight species have bred here in this temporary haven. Access to the docks is limited to official users and special permission is needed to view them thoroughly but there are several vantage points always available, especially from the bridges crossing the dock entrances. The birds may often be seen on their flight lines from the docks to other feeding grounds on the river.

There are greater dockland adventures in store. The proposals for the redevelopment of London Docks include a new woodland at Wapping.

The river is the city, the lifeblood of the place. It gave it its origin, its meaning and its greatness. On its gravel terraces grew up the twin Cities of London and Westminster. So important was it in commerce, in transport, in water supply that the City of London claimed control as far upstream as Staines and downstream to the Medway. Boundary stones bearing the City arms can be found by Staines Bridge and along the Medway, at Upnor, for example. The urban growth of London has now reached and even overtaken those ancient limits, and the administrative boundaries of Greater London, reflecting the realities of the present, stretch from Hampton to Dartford.

Not only is the river the City's grandest open space but it brings the feel of the open countryside, from Cotswolds and Chilterns into the metropolis. Twice a day the tide brings the salt and sea smells from the North Sea. At any time the river is of absorbing interest but in winter it is full of the sights and sounds of birds, of wintering wildfowl and waders from the Baltic and the Arctic, finding warmth and feeding grounds much to their taste. So long a foul, open sewer, the Thames is now a highway for birds and fish.

Even at a time when salmon was part of the staple diet of the fishing villages like Wapping and Woolwich, the pollution of the river was already a problem but nothing as compared with the effects of the growth of industrialisation and housing that followed the dockland developments of the early nineteenth century. The result was cholera and the Big Stink of 1856 that even led to a walk-out in Parliament. The Thames Conservancy was set up in the following year and the long, slow process of cleaning up began. The man whose name appears on plaques on the Victoria Embankment, Sir Joseph Bazalgette, is the real hero of the Thames. He was also responsible for the new sewage system that took London's outfall far down the Thames by pipeline to Crossness and to Beckton. But the tide brought the sewage upstream every day. The oxygen content at Woolwich, for example, was still officially zero as recently as 1947. It was not until new treatment plants were installed at the outfalls and new legislation passed to prevent pollution upstream that the river began to recover. By 1967, twenty species of fish were recorded in the river. By 1977, forty-one, with sea-horses at Dagenham, sea trout off Deptford and a salmon at West Thurrock, the first on the river for more than one hundred years. The Chinese mitten crab was found at Chelsea and flounders, scads, smelt, sprats and eels were appearing in abundance. The oxygen content had reached the target of 30 per cent, necessary for salmon.

There are parts of the river that nearly justify the praises of a survey in 1625 that were sung for 'a sweete, cleare and pleasante river'.[1] From Putney Bridge upstream to Kingston and Hampton the Thames retains some of the aspects of a river in the countryside, with a tow-path walk almost uninterrupted on the south side. It's a walk for boots rather than light shoes for the river often laps over the banks when winter rains from the 4,000 square miles of catchment meet the incoming tide. The open spaces, parks, playing fields, commons and gardens seem to outnumber the built-up stretches of the shore and the old riverside settlements can still be identified with their medieval churches at their centres. Many were the old landing places, the

5

Saxon hythes, a name that occurs, much corrupted, in place names. Chelsea was the chalk hythe, Lambeth, the lamb hythe, Rotherhithe, the landing stage for cattle, Erith, the gravelly hythe. Putney was Putta's hythe and Stepney, the hythe of a Saxon called Stebba. There is a signpost near the Mansion House in the centre of the City that points to Garlickhythe, one of London's most ancient quays.

Another common element is 'ey', meaning 'island' which occurs in Battersea and Bermondsey and Thorney, the island on which Westminster was founded.

Two of these old villages face each other on opposite sides of Putney Bridge. On the Putney side, the church of St Mary is in a sad state of disrepair in a riverside that is otherwise spick and span. All Saints at Fulham, in contrast, stands in a fine setting of garden and parkland by the Bishop's palace. This is one of London's lesser-known gems. The riverside embankment walk leads to inner grounds and courtyards which are open to the public all the year round. A Tudor gateway leads to a vine-clad cloister. The botanical garden, a rare survival, is only open in the summer months, sufficient enticement for a return visit. Even in winter, the collection of trees, especially the holm oaks, gives pleasure enough. In Tudor times, the place was famous for its herons and spoonbills. Herons are still seen along the river but spoonbills are almost unknown. I say 'almost' for there is a recent record of a spoonbill seen at Richmond.

Alongside the Bishop's palace was another fine country seat called Craven Cottage. The name has achieved new fame as the home of the local football team, now one of the many playing fields along the banks which attracts its quota of gulls.

One day the tow-path from Putney may be part of a new long-distance walkway that will lead upstream to the headwaters of the Thames but for the moment the Londoner must be content with a good day's walking and watching which can lead, if the flesh is willing, as far as London's upstream boundary. The walker may be envious of the scullers and rowers who move with deceptive ease along the river. But even more dexterous is the cormorant that flies downstream close to the water surface and comes to rest in mid-stream just above Putney Bridge. It faces downstream, its body almost hidden in the water, its long black neck upright as a periscope. Then it dips easily into the water, submerges for nearly half a minute before surfacing with a fish wriggling in its mouth. The fish is swallowed with the minimum of effort and, after a pause of about ten seconds, the cormorant dives again. In a quarter of an hour, the bird spent more time under the water than above it and ate upwards of twenty fish.

I always think of Northumberland's rocky coasts when I see cormorants, remembering them plummetting from the cliffs of the Farnes. The first cormorants introduced to St James's Park in 1888 were brought from the Farnes. Now cormorants are regular winter visitors all along the river. There is a roost of more than a dozen of them in the trees by the river bank at Syon Park.

Just upstream from Putney, occupying the great bend of the river is the reservoir of Barn Elms, tantalisingly out of view behind its retaining walls. This is one of the largest gathering grounds for birds in London, especially gulls. Special permission is needed to enter the area for bird-watching but the bird life spills out over the surrounding area.

Gulls' flight lines have been plotted over London, usually following the Thames and its tributaries such as the Colne, and many of those paths converge on the large inland reservoirs like Barn Elms. Their aerial highways lead from their feeding grounds which are often the rubbish tips all round London. With the city turning out more than four million tons of rubbish each year there are plenty of pickings for the gulls and other scavengers. Some gulls still fly to the estuaries but many have become land birds in all but name.

They are so tame and widespread now that it is extraordinary to read W.H. Hudson's study of birds in London written at the end of the last century when the gulls first began to roost at Barn Elms and the crowds lined the bridges to watch them. 'The marvellous flight and power of wing of the gull came as an absolute revelation', he wrote.[2] And that was the last time people shot the gulls. After that they began to feed them! The gulls first came in after a series of hard winters and then stayed to enjoy the mild ones. One of the most common gulls in January is the black-headed gull, though its head may not be quite black in winter plumage, but there is the herring gull, the commonest of the coastal gulls, with a heavy yellow bill. The biggest are the black-backed gulls, easily identified, both the greater and the lesser, with their impressive size and wing span. Wintering inland may also be some of the less common species such as the glaucous gull and the common gull. By the 1950s more than 100,000 gulls were recorded in the London area and in recent years this number has more than doubled. It is possible that new methods of disposing of rubbish such as incineration may cut down their feeding grounds and cause a lowering of numbers but for the moment they are amongst the most numerous birds in the city. Their vociferous cries bring a touch of the seaside even to suburban rooftops.

Beyond Hammersmith Bridge, the tow-path broadens out through a belt of trees, with some willows of great girth, and thorny shrubs, giving cover to many of the smaller land birds, especially the pied wagtail. A pleasant row of houses and a church spire announce Chiswick on the north bank followed by the green spaces of Duke's Meadows and Barnes Bridge. Barnes is typical of those places that manage to keep their own character with houses surviving from the days of their rural independence and some memorable inns with salty names. Once you start on this route, it is very difficult to turn back. Every bend of the river beckons. Beyond lies Kew and Syon and the picturesque stretch of Strand-on-the-Green cheek by jowl with the warehouses of the Brentford Basin. Past Richmond with its elegant eighteenth-century bridge, the oldest on the London stretch of the river, the riverbank is lined with the magnificent villas of the past. The river was the jewel in their crown. So, rightly, the statue of the river god reclines in classic ease on the forecourt of Ham House.

He can be a wrathful god, for the stretch upstream from Ham to Teddington is particularly vulnerable to flooding. The riverside wall at Isleworth records the highest floods of the last two hundred years. Given heavy rainfal running off the land upstream, a high tide and a strong north wind driving the North Sea waters into the estuary, the effect is felt right up to Teddington Lock.

The palaces and noble seats that lined the reaches beyond Putney once had their counterparts nearer the City of Westminster when Battersea, Chelsea and Lambeth were still riverside villages set amongst marsh, meadow and market garden until late in the eighteenth century. The area had its famous (or infamous) gardens, notorious pleasure grounds like Vauxhall and Ranelegh. Ranelegh is part of the green space in front of the Royal Hospital at Chelsea, and Vauxhall is lost beneath one of the least interesting parts of the riverside. There is still a small park at Vauxhall some way from the original site that was opened in the 1890s as the result of the efforts of Octavia Hill, one of a select band of Victorian philanthropists, a pioneer of the open-space movement and, eventually, of the National Trust, who was to make the city a much more pleasant place than it would otherwise have been. Vauxhall Park may not look exceptional now, just a typical recreation area with tree-lined walks, lawns, and playground for children but when it was opened, Octavia wrote of it,

> For long years, as long as our people need it and wish for it, flowers will grow there and sunlight have leave to penetrate and no wheels will make dust or noise there but, near their homes, the old may rest and the young play and Spring after Spring the golden crocuses shall teach how bright life comes out of the dark earth after the winter chill.[3]

Such was the spirit and vision behind the formation of London's parks. Writing at a time when London's rapid growth was devouring its surrounding countryside, people like Octavia Hill fought to preserve at least a vestige of the countryside inside the city. The vision gives new point to a winter perambulation from Battersea to Chelsea, completing the circuit by two tree-lined embankments and two bridges, Albert and Battersea.

Battersea Fields were covered with market gardens and swampy wastes, the common fields of the village, the site of fairs, racing and other sports, wild enough to be used as a duelling ground, the most famous duel being between the Duke of Wellington and the Marquis of Winchelsea. Colonel Blood once hid in the rushes there in an attempt to assassinate Charles II who enjoyed bathing in the Thames at Chelsea. Yet 'a place out of Hell that surpassed Sodom and Gomorrah' was transformed into the most popular open-air resort in the metropolis. By an Act of Parliament in 1846 the decision was made to create a new royal park on the south bank about two hundred acres in extent. With the aid of material excavated from the new Victoria Dock extension, the marshes were filled in and landscaped with mounds and low hills to give variety to the scene. Avenues of elm and plane were planted, a subtropical garden and an alpine garden laid out but the centre piece was a long serpentine lake. That lake has as good a collection of water fowl as you will find in London, with the common species like mallard, coot, moorhen, gulls and Canada geese being joined by black swans, bean geese, shelduck, pochard and tufted duck. W.H. Hudson described Battersea as one of the best bird-watching areas in London, being on the flight-path of many migrating and wintering species. The lake is backed by a variety of trees and shrubs, an enclosure with deer, goats and cranes and, at the far end, by many mature trees planted in the subtropical garden. A park of great variety, it culminates at the west end in an old English garden with some flowers still in bloom, the rose of Sharon and the broom, both with gay yellow flowers. The box trees are just showing the first hint of tiny white flowers that will break as the days lengthen.

Across the Albert Bridge stands Chelsea Old Church, the heart of the riverside settlement where Sir Thomas More had one of his country seats. His statue stands in front of the church. Alongside is the sunken Roper Garden and a fifteenth century manor house brought from Bishopsgate in the City in 1910, its white stonework contrasting with the red brick of the surrounding houses. Moving back to the east, the Embankment Gardens stand in front of Cheyne Walk and the site of one of Henry VIII's manor houses. A plaque informs us that mulberry trees planted in the reign of Elizabeth I still survive in one of the back gardens, which makes them much older than the mulberry at Charlton House in south-east London that claims to be the first planted in England, in 1608.

When the great Tudor families lived here, the river lapped against their gardens and orchards. The Chelsea Embankment was started in 1871 and the Albert Embankment on the south side in the 1860s. The embankment of Battersea Park was amongst the first of its kind that began the control of the errant, flooding river. Now the river has been narrowed and flows more swiftly, we shall have no more frost fairs like the one of 1814, though the river did freeze over above Teddington in the great winter of 1963. You are most aware of this change in the river's fortunes at Westminster where the Queen's steps, designed by Sir Christopher Wren, stand at the approach to Whitehall, about 86 yards from the present embankment. Close by, in the Embankment Gardens near Villiers Street, is one of the Watergates where the water reached the gardens along the Strand, the riverside road that linked the two cities of Westminster and London.

A garden of supreme interest still survives from the pre-embankment days, the Chelsea Physic Garden. An old plaque in the new boundary wall bears the inscription 'Hortus Botanicus

Societatis Pharmaceuticae Lond. 1686'. Within the wall is one of the finest collections of medicinal and culinary herbs in the country, founded by the Worshipful Society of Apothecaries. This was the centre for 'herberising' expeditions into the surrounding countryside for the instruction of the students. Still the centre of botanical research, the garden is occasionally open to the public but much can be seen in winter from the riverside gateway as the screening trees are bare. The embankment walk back towards Battersea Bridge then passes the wide green lawns of the Royal Hospital famous for its Chelsea pensioners, another open space with ample cover for birds. The route then crosses the river back into Battersea Park.

Throughout the walk the dominant tree is the London plane, easily recognisable because of its flaking bark which helps it to appear ever fresh despite the city atmosphere. The London plane is a hybrid between the oriental plane and the American plane, otherwise known as the buttonwood. Its leaf is very similar to that of the sycamore. It was first introduced in the seventeenth century and was already planted up-river at Barnes by 1680. Its roots can function well in the restricted compacted soils of the city and being root firm is not likely to be blown down. It comprises well over half the planted trees of central London. One of its winter characteristics is the fat seed pod hanging down like a spiky ball waiting to spatter on the pavements and find a new lodging place. I have a magnificent specimen outside my window, higher than a four-storey house, a regular perch for sparrows, tits and finches, wagtails, and a tawny owl and a roost for starlings. Even those planted three hundred years ago are still growing strongly and the century-old trees along the embankments have not yet reached their full maturity. With care they will give pleasure to many city generations yet.

One of the great pioneers of botany and gardening has an unusual memorial downstream from Battersea at Lambeth. In the now redundant church of St Mary's alongside the Archbishop's palace is a window recalling the Tradescants, father and son. Their tomb stands in the small churchyard, opposite the Houses of Parliament, along that of Bligh of the Bounty. The inscription tells their story, men who 'lived till they had travelled Art and Nature through' in the search for new plants. Ultimately they themselves were 'transplanted' and changed 'this garden for a paradise.' John Tradescant, senior, began as a gardener in the Kentish village of

Meopham and became the royal gardener to Charles I and one of the most famous collectors of his or any other time. The Tradescant Trust is making the garden into a living memorial, replanting the herbs, shrubs and trees that the seventeenth-century pioneers first introduced, such as the tulip tree and the laburnum. When Tradescant was at Lambeth, he was in the very centre of the market garden area in the drained marshes of the south bank, made fruitful in part by the Flemish immigrants of the seventeenth century.

The spirit of riverside gardens is not quite dead. In an unlikely spot, tucked in between empty warehouses, new hotels and Tower Bridge, opposite the Tower of London, a three-acre site has been set aside for a new ecological garden in a conscious attempt to reintroduce the countryside to a part of London that is singularly lacking in green spaces. The wish is to give both flora and fauna a chance to establish a roothold and a foothold in inner London.

The last of London's marshes lies a long way down river past the main dock area towards Erith on the south side and Rainham on the north shore. Even here the pressure for building space has changed one of the most extensive marshes, once the grazing areas for the sheep flocks belonging to the monks of Lessness Abbey, into the new town of Thamesmead. On the same marsh is the main southern outfall of London's sewage system at Crossness. The northern outfall lies across the river, together with rifle ranges that make access difficult. Yet this area downstream from Woolwich has become one of the most important areas for wintering wildfowl in Europe, with more than 10,000 birds recorded, making it a wetland of international significance. The sewage outfalls attract rather than repel the birds and the increasing purity of the water and its marine life has led to an annual increase in the number and variety of birds recorded. More than a dozen of these remnant marshes have been designated as Sites of Special Scientific Interest. They are under constant pressure for new industrial development but for the moment they give Londoners the chance of seeing masses of birds that would once have been typical of the further shores of Essex, Kent and Sussex.

There is a public right of way from Erith along the river wall to the Crossness outfall and patches of pastures and drainage ditches still remain. Artificial lakes run right up to the towering blocks and houses of Thamesmead, attracting wintering birds right up to the windows. The most accessible place to give the real flavour of the open estuary is at Crayford Ness on the easternmost boundary of London. Moat Lane leads from Slade Green station out to the banks of the river Cray passing a farm by a medieval moated site that still retains its stone walls, though the brick building within the moat is now a ruin. At low tide, herons stalk along the edge of the muddy shore and stonechats perch boldly on the dead heads of bristly ox-tongue with quick flights to the ground to feed. Oyster catchers patrol the river while snipe, reed buntings and finches busy themselves in the few remaining ditches that bisect the pastures around the intrusive industrial site. A pity one piece of marshland could not have been left untouched. Out on the estuary, flocks of shelduck and mallard float on the tide. The mallard are already pairing off, bobbing up and down in ritual courtship. As the frost rises from the ground, the starling flocks work across the pasture and lapwings come down to feed on leatherjackets and other insects. Even in this restricted area, a good two or three miles circuit is available using the river wall. Across the river are the Aveley saltings, the main high-tide roost for waders. Mallard, teal, wigeon, pintails, tufted duck, redshank and ringed plover have all been present in their hundreds while flocks of more than a thousand dunlin, shelduck and pochard may be seen. And heard. The sound of the birds is as exciting as the sight, all one with the lapping water and the ships streaming up the estuary. At West Thurrock, dunlin numbers have reached more than seven thousand, just outside the London area. The major bird-watching area for the specialists is undoubtedly the Rainham marshes at the mouth of the Beam and Ingrebourne rivers, only a mile south of the main A13 trunk road.

The main access point is by way of Ferry Lane at Rainham which leads to a right-of-way along the river wall. No one could call this a pleasant piece of countryside but the birds love it. A farmer from Aberdeen runs a large flock of Welsh sheep on what is left of the marshland grazing and manages, despite the pressures of industry, pollution and people, to win regular prizes at the Smith-field Show for his livestock. Striding along the river wall with his crooked stick, he brings the true country image to this extraordinary area where vast acres of London rubbish are being used to reclaim the marsh. As each lorry load falls in a steaming heap so the massed birds descend. The great black-backed gulls are the kings of the garbage and take first picking. Then come the mobs of other gulls, the carrion crows, the starlings, the sparrows and dunnocks darkening the sky above the dumper trucks. Along the two-mile walk to Coldharbour Point, the flocks of finches and buntings fly before you. Chaffinches, yellowhammers, goldfinches, meadow pipits, pied wagtails, greenfinches, reed buntings search for appropriate pickings. A solitary stonechat perches on a red post, black head, red breast like a memory of summer heaths. Out on the estuary there is a gathering of mallard and shelduck and two cormorants feeding on the incoming tide. Oyster-catchers hurtle along the shore with cries of alarm and a dozen snipe zig-zag out of danger. Sanderlings potter along the mud-flats, their bellies gleaming white. During migrations this area attracts many of the rarer birds like the black-tailed godwit, the spotted redshank and the spoonbill.

Even on a January day, the leaves of the sea-aster are fleshy and green while the bristly ox-tongue is often in flower. Some areas of phragmites grow in the ditches and other seed-bearing plants abound. The main foods for the wildfowl are the worms, notably the tubifex worm and the ragworm but also green algae, some fish and grain spillage from the mills. The increasing purification of the water has caused a change in the location of the tubifex worms which have thrived in brackish water with a low oxygen content. No one is quite sure what the effect of the new Thames barrier, now being constructed near Woolwich, will be but the birds have a happy way of adapting just as long as feeding grounds are available. The wildlife of the estuary is sufficiently important to be taken into consideration for any future plans for the area. It has been suggested, for example, that the shoreline around Barking Bay and Creek would make a country park with a difference, a sanctuary at the mouth of the river Roding, where as many as a thousand swans have been seen at one time.

This influx of birds affects all the sand and gravel pits that abound on the Essex shore and the reservoirs of the London area such as Walthamstow along the Lea Valley where cormorants, shags and heron are quite common. One of the most famous assembly places is the Brent, otherwise known as the Welsh Harp, close by the Edgware Road past Dollis Hill, an urban sanctuary if ever there was one. The regular visitors top the fifty mark and with vagrants and rarer species added the total may reach over one hundred.

The River

London's oldest and most important open space, the Thames is now the highway for an invasion of wildlife that adds in incomparable measure to the variety of the city's life.

Highgate Cemetery

2
THE CITY

As February breaks, the snowdrops are already opening out their small white bells in the churchyard of St Paul's. Candlemas, the second day of the month, is the traditional date for their flowering, the medieval festival of the Presentation, the presentation of the male child forty days after his birth. The snowdrop, symbol of purity and virginity, was strewn on altars. Flowering so early in the year, it often lacks the help of bees and other insects in its fertilisation so, as the small drop opens and matures, it sheds its own cloud of pollen for self-fertilisation to take place, another virgin symbol. Although naturalised here for centuries, the flower is still most common in gardens and churchyards. Gerard, the Elizabethan herbalist, who had his herb garden in Holborn, commented that the snowdrop grew wild in Italy. It was probably introduced to this country by the religious orders for ceremonial purposes such as Candlemas, its pure whiteness defying the prevalent gloom of the season.

'A welcome sight', said a voice behind me, in a strong East End accent. The ex-docker told me he spent all his time roaming the City streets. As we talked, it became obvious that he knew every open space, park and garden in the City, including the most secluded ones such as St Ethelburga's, accessible only through the medieval church jammed between the shops and offices of Bishopsgate. We joined in admiration of the first of the camellias opening in front of the Bank of America nearby, and agreed that the daffodils at Great St Helen's would not be long. They usually break out of their protective green sheaths about the middle of the month a full thirty days before they would be flowering out in the Darent valley,

17

beyond London's urban rim. Spring comes almost as early in the City as it does in Cornwall. London's 'heat island' is as effective as the warm waters of the North Atlantic Drift. The tall buildings, the brick walls, the central heating and the shelter from cold winds all have their effect, raising the temperature by more than one degree centigrade. That doesn't sound much but it's about the same difference as the average temperatures of February and March. When it's February in the country, it's March in the City, so to speak. The night temperatures at the centre can be as much as seven degrees higher than the outermost suburbs. So the City gives its flora a longer growing season and greater freedom from frost. But the tall buildings create caverns of darkness, too, though the daffodils we both mentioned were in a tub by a north-facing wall. Spotting the first snowdrop and the first daffodil is as obsessive as hearing the first cuckoo and just as deserving of a letter to *The Times*.

The high temperatures and low humidity also have the advantage of preventing really thick fogs. Dickensian London is a thing of the past. The dense pea-soupers that always seemed to shroud the horrors of Seven Dials no longer affect the City, for it was the first area to have a clean air policy, in 1954. So for a gentle winter climate, if you cannot afford the Riviera, join the wintering birds in the heart of London. Put on your boots and walk into town and tour the churchyards and the windowboxes to meet the spring flowers.

My East End companion joined me in a stroll round the churchyard. A familiar plaque told an unfamiliar story. In 1878, the churchyard space of the Cathedral Church of St Paul's was combined with those of St Gregory-by-St Paul's and St Faith-the-Virgin-under-St Paul's to make the present garden, enlarged during the City redevelopment in 1966. There is a new rose garden, the flowers growing up the dead poles of birch. Some of the heathers were cheerfully in flower but best of all were clumps of witchhazel with their ragged yellow petals on leafless twigs. The iron railings about the yard gave us a direct link with the Wealden countryside, for the iron was forged near Lamberhurst in the Gloucester furnace, using Kentish ore, timber and water power. But my companion had eyes for the trees, so varied in species as to make a miniature arboretum. There was maple and lime, gingko and plane, ash and willow-leaved pear, cherry, sweet gum bearing the delicious name of liquidamber, then whitebeam and mulberry. 'Don't park your car there in September' he warned. He explained that the mulberry fruits are so prolific that they stain the pavements and everything else a dark purple. 'No one picks them now', he said, with the voice of a man for whom things are never quite as good as they were. All round the churchyard, new trees were being planted, mostly red-twigged limes. It was almost a surprise to find the native beech planted to the north-east of the yard but even they were accompanied by dwarf palms. The exotic trees seem to do better than the native deciduous trees that must have grown here before the city was founded.

In those far-off times when London first achieved a name, perhaps before the Romans established their bridgehead, oak forest covered the heavy clay soils of the London Basin. The gravel terraces of Thames-side, on which the City grew, would have been more lightly wooded, perhaps with birch and willow and hazel. Oak trees and other native deciduous trees are rare in the City now. So too are conifers, and evergreens, the churchyard yew, for example, being notable by its absence. There are something like 2,000 trees planted in the City and they are mostly introduced species. The most popular are the London plane, the Norway maple, the lime, the whitebeam, the catalpa, the cherry and the acacia. We have already encountered the catalpa and its long dangling seed-pods on the Embankment Gardens. It was introduced from North America in 1726 and develops in due season, an enormous spade-shaped leaf. The trees are not only chosen for their decorative characteristics, the bark of the acacia, the berries of the whitebeam, the flowers of the lime, the leaves of the gingko, but for their ability to survive, even thrive, in the urban atmosphere. Even with comparatively clean air, it is remarkable that trees like the catalpa, the Indian bean tree, more at home in the American mid-West, should look so healthy. The gingko, of which there are at least two in St Paul's churchyard, is one of the oldest order of all living trees. Its fossilised leaves have been found in coal measures which gives it an inheritance of at least 250 million years. It survives in the wild only in a limited area of China but is a feature of eastern formal gardens. Its small, fan-shaped leaves, bright green when they emerge, are reminiscent of the maidenhair fern, so the tree is also known as the maidenhair tree. Identifying the trees of the 'City arboretum' is challenge enough. Finding the native deciduous species is even

19

more of an adventure. The site of the nearest oak tree to St Paul's could be a useful addition to any quiz programme.

Churchyards are all-important in the City. Apart from the river itself, they are the most important open spaces remaining in the heart of the metropolis. Judging by City rents, every blade of grass there must be the most expensive in Britain. As one of the Victorian pioneers affirmed, every garden in the City is twice a garden. Medieval London had 139 churches, most with burial grounds much smaller than the traditional God's acre. There wasn't room. There was only one square mile available for all purposes. Fire, blitz, war and, most important, the loss of a resident population has reduced the number to forty-seven. Their churchyards comprise nearly half of the total open spaces in the City of London. Altogether there are over a hundred open spaces maintained by the Corporation, varying from the eight acres in the Barbican redevelopment to a mere triangle inches wide on Snow Hill, still wide enough to have its trees, shrubs and official plaque.

As London grew and the inhabitants moved further and further out, leaving the City to become a desert on Sundays, many churches became redundant. The space was potentially valuable and the first attempts were made to destroy some of the churches. The neglect of the yards was mentioned by Dickens. He saw an elderly couple making hay with a rake 'gravely among the graves!' The Burials Act of 1852 permitted the closure of the yards and no more burials would take place in the City. Fortunately, there was a growing awareness of the need for the preservation and increase of open spaces that had resulted, for example, in the creation of Battersea Park. A group of determined idealists, amongst them the sisters Miranda and Octavia Hill, formed the Kyrle Society 'for the diffusion of beauty' and one of the forms that beauty should take was in green spaces, however small, to become, as Octavia called them, 'open air sitting rooms for the poor'.[1] She was acutely aware of the loss of the countryside from the daily life of the people and wanted consciously to protect it, in common and heath and park within reach of people. 'I shall care most for small central spaces',[2] she wrote and the spaces she saw as potential recreation areas were the churchyards. A series of acts of parliament between 1855 and 1884 protected the churchyards, forbade buildings upon them and made them available as recreational areas, culminating in the formation in 1882 of the Metropolitan Public Garden Association. From that date on, the list of churchyards so transformed grew encouragingly, in the East End, too, St Dunstan's in Stepney, St Anne's at Limehouse, St Bartholomew's, Bethnal Green, St Paul's, Shadwell. So important was this movement at the time that the opening of St Paul's churchyard at Rotherhithe, south of the river, was carried out by two princesses and a duchess. Amongst the thousands walking daily up Charing Cross Road or St Martin's Lane to the junction with Oxford Street, there are very few who will take a turn through the churchyard of St Giles-in-the-Fields. Yet that churchyard is just about the only green reminder of the fields the church stood in, apart from unexpectedly countryfied names like Long Acre and Hop Garden off St Martin's Lane, where Parkinson had his seventeenth-century herb garden. It was also one of the pioneer achievements of the open-space movement. When the outdoor sitting room was laid out, it was alongside one of the most congested, corners of Dickensian London, the notorious Seven Dials. A small garden, a children's playground, some trees and wooden seats may not seem very significant now. A hundred years ago they added up to a vision.

The Victorian vision was based on a medieval reality. Norman London, according to the contemporary account by William Fitzstephen, was full of 'citizens gardens and orchards planted with trees', especially along the Strand between the Cities of London and Westminster and round the walls of London. The gardens of the religious orders formed part of the green halo, the Minories to the east, the Whitefriars, Blackfriars, Charterhouse and St John's of Clerkenwell to the west. The Bishop of Ely had an orchard near his palace at Holborn close by the present Plumtree Court. In later years, there were herb gardens like those at Chelsea and the Bishop's palace at Fulham close by the City. Gerard had his garden at Holborn. The Earl of Lincoln grew apples, pears, nuts and cherries, beans, onions, garlic, leeks, vines and roses in his gardens which occupied part of the land now covered by Lincoln's Inn Fields.

Not only were there gardens and orchards within the City, the open countryside reached to the walls themselves. Ten minutes walk from St Paul's brought the citizens to the open fields. 'On the north side', wrote Fitzstephen, 'are pastures and plain meadows, with brooks running through them, turning watermills with a pleasant noise. Not far off is a great forest, a well-wooded chase, having good covert for harts, bucks, does, boars and wild bulls.'[3] We can measure this twelfth-century word picture with the visual images of Ralph Agas's map of Tudor London on display in the Guildhall Library. There are trees in the Temple, horses at Smithfield, a tenter-ground for stretching cloth by the Tower. A fen lies by the Minories and gardens line the walls. Clerkenwell is still a village and St Martin's really in the fields with farmland at Charing Cross.

We walk the City streets now and conjure with names that recall the past when town and country were so closely linked. Poultry, Cheapside, Milk Street, Wood Street, Bread Street, Garlic Hill, Cornhill, Grassmarket, Plough Court. Now we have to be thankful for churchyards and window-boxes. Many of the displays of flowers and shrubs bear the signs showing the approval of the Worshipful Company of Gardeners. Since 1963 the Company has been active in encouraging a greener, more colourful City, giving a direct link with the medieval past, for the Gardeners' Company was set up by royal charter in 1605, 'the craft or mystery of gardening, planting, setting, sowing, cutting, arboring, rocking, mounting, covering, fencing and removing of plants, herbs, seeds, fruits, trees, stocks, sets'.[4] The mystery lives on, 'for their life is altogether in the fields or gardens'. Their lives are in the City, as well.

A plaque to the Gardeners' Company in the churchyard of St Dunstan's-in-the-East asserts that their origins lie far beyond the seventeenth-century charter, being mentioned as early as the thirteenth century. The company supplied most of the flowers for this serene place opened in 1967. Destroyed in the 1666 fire and again by the wartime bombing, the church was left as ruin and now the deserted nave and the tower form the backdrop of a formal garden. A weeping willow occupies the north entrance and the fig tree by the south wall bears small, green fruits that may eventually ripen. Within minutes of us entering that garden, the pigeons and sparrows were down. Wherever you may be in the City on the quietest of winter week-ends, the birds will seek you out. The sparrow and the pigeon are the two most successful urban colonists. The urban pigeon is a descendant of the rock dove which found its natural habitat in rock faces. Man builds artificial cliffs, complete with parapets and roofs as nesting sites and roosts and the pigeons move in. They tend to congregate around the markets, the riverside and the docks looking for grain, seeds and grit for their capacious diet. So successful are they, that they may be responsible for a decline in the number of sparrows. Once they were persecuted and pigeon pie had its charms, but now they waddle and strut in every street and space, cropping the seeds from shepherd's purse growing in the cracks of pavements and investigating every discarded paper bag. I have even seen a pigeon dunking a bread crust in a puddle before eating it. They breed all the year round. The male with ruff bristling moving in ritual circles in sight of his mate is as common in February as at any other time. Both the feral pigeon and the wood pigeon breed in the City, the wood pigeon being the larger of the species, big, plump and bold. Also known as the ring dove, it stalks bright-eyed through the streets. Ringing has shown, that, like the sparrow, pigeons seldom move more than half a mile from their home base. They are as parochial as cockneys.

The sparrow more readily wears his cockney title. Most numerous when horses trotted the streets and nose bags and feed troughs gave the sparrows a liberal helping, the 'passer domesticus', the house sparrow, nests in buildings as well as trees, shrubs and hedges. It achieves an even higher density in the urban areas than it does in the country. The slightly larger dunnock, with sharper beak and slatey colouration may also be seen in the City though it is much rarer. One of the most familiar sounds is the 'shindie' of a congregation of sparrows, hundreds of them chattering away in their 'chapels', their favoured roosting sites in shrubs or an old tree. They adapt to anything showing a great interest, for example, in overflow pipes. I watched a mob attacking the tin foil wrapping of a pie, jumping to and fro on its shiny surface, pecking determinedly, retreating hurriedly from the metallic response. One bold character remained seeming to admire its reflection in the foil. The sparrows are usually the first birds to be bold enough to perch on the hand to feed. They have an easier life than their hedge-sparrow brethren out in the rural belt coping with frozen ground, frozen ponds and sub-zero temperatures. London's heat island is as encouraging to birds as it is to the flora, stimulating grubs and worms to early activity.

The sparrow and the pigeon are not the only breeding species in the inner City. The blackbird, the starling, the pied wagtail and the goldfinch are all recorded here. Even the kestrel finds the concrete cliffs and canyons to its liking with rodents and birds like the sparrow as its major food supply. The birds may have a lean time at the week-ends when the City is like a desert but even then there are honeypots where the visitors gather, especially the Tower of London and there the birds congregate in force, meeting up with the pied wagtails patrolling the river front and the wildfowl moving upstream into the inner docks like St Katherine's and London Docks close by the Tower.

When the Norman Tower was built it stood between the City and the countryside. To the east was marshy ground and a stream called the Langbourne fed from the springs at Fenchurch, running through the pastures and tenter ground of East Smithfield. Beyond were the Saxon parishes of Wapping and Stepney with their ploughland, meadows, pastures, mills and woodland for five hundred pigs. The Domesday record showed woodland pannage stretching from here across the Lea into Essex.

Both within the Tower and without there are fragments of the medieval wall built on Roman foundations. London's clay could supply material for brick-making but there was no good building stone nearby so the Wall and other early structures depended on ragstone and flint brought from Kent by river. Most of the stone was hewn from quarries along the Medway, in the vicinity of Maidstone. By those broken walls eight ravens hobble and hop, tugging at pieces of meat. Once ravens were scavengers of the city streets but this is their last sanctuary. London's most famous birds, the stock is maintained by bringing in birds from the Highlands and from Cornwall. Six must be kept by royal prerogative so eight are maintained just in case. If the ravens leave, the Tower falls. The largest of the crow family, they are fed twice a day. 'The only real beef-eaters round here, now', said one of the colourful guards with a chuckle. One of the birds has been known to live for more than forty years. Two of them sat on a railing on Tower Green cawing at the window of one of the period houses that give this grim place the look of a village green. The ravens, which can eat small birds, seemed indifferent to the eight house sparrows, fifteen starlings and five pigeons that hovered around their feeding area under the shadow of the White Tower.

The neat, green spaces round the Tower, its lawns and moats, last filled during the floods of January 1928, combined with Trinity

Gardens to the north and the grounds of All Hallows Barking-by-the-Tower to the west make one of the City's largest open spaces, more than two and a half acres originally maintained by the Metropolitan Public Gardens Association, founded after the Metropolitan Open Spaces Act of 1881. The imaginative impulse that protected that open space a century ago has been perpetuated in the lay-out of St Katherine's Dock as a marina, a place of unusual shapes and sounds, Thames barges and the Nore lightship alongside cannons and warehouses, a happy conjunction of land and sea that points to the whole essence of London. It was the 'fishful river of Thames with his ebbing and flowing,' that, according to Fitzstephen 'hath long since subverted them', that is to say, the riverside walls.[5] The landward side remains in fragments and we could follow them northwards along the Minories by Goodman's Yard to Aldgate but I prefer a parallel route by way of Seething Lane and its snowdrops and fine trees on the site of Samuel Pepys' old navy office. Past St Olave's, a rare pre-fire church and one of the best in London, up Crutched Friars, a street as crooked as the name suggests, out to Aldgate and Aldgate High Street. Look east along the broad tree-lined thoroughfare. That is yet another tribute to Octavia Hill who inspired the tree-planting to create an East End boulevard. The road to the north, Houndsditch, literally was the defensive ditch in front of the City wall. At either end stands a church dedicated to St Botolph; both of them 'without', that is without the wall. The frequent dedication to the same saint is one of the reasons for the double-barrelled naming of most City churches and their yards. We have left All Hallows Barking-by-the-Tower behind and will soon pass All Hallows-on-the-Wall. St Botolph's-without-Aldgate leads to St Botolph's-without-Bishopsgate. The latter churchyard contains an infant school with seventeenth-century statues by the door, wearing Puritan dress. The churchyard has a well-tended garden with many hawthorn and spring flowers emerging. The City's newest garden, laid out for the Queen's jubilee in 1977 lies close-by in Houndsditch, in Cavendish Court with trees and shurbs donated by City companies and guilds. It has more of the Venetian piazza about it than the older spaces but at least it makes a break from the office blocks.

Bishopsgate was famous for its medieval gardens having some of the finest out-of-town residences. They lie beneath Liverpool

Street station and Spitalfields Market, the latter with its fruit and vegetables and flowers offering some sort of historical continuum.

Through St Botolph's churchyard, we reach All Hallows on-the-Wall, one of the many spaces little bigger than a sitting room but replete with seat, grass and shrubs. London Wall leads to the west but we must make a short diversion along Throgmorton Avenue to a small garden by the Draper's Hall which sports a grove of mulberry trees, once part of a large garden created by Thomas Cromwell. The Drapers used to supply the Lord Mayor with mulberry pie once a year from their own trees. Return to the Wall and we are in Circus Place and Finsbury Gardens, the largest open space in the City and best reminder of the open, marshy moorland that gave its name to Moorgate and to the medieval citizens their greatest country pleasures.

The Romans, with their usual practical skill, culverted the streams flowing from the north towards the northern ramparts of the Wall. Neglect of the culverts and drainage channels turned the area into an ill-drained area of meadows and marshes, frozen over in winter to the delight of skaters, and, in summer, the quickest access to the countryside. The great fen was partly drained and bridged in Henry VIII's reign and archery encouraged. Three windmills were erected on mounds of cattle dung. The pressure for cottages, country villas and enclosures threatened the City's playground. Complaints were made that there was not even room for stock to be driven into the markets. Enclosures of the common fields of the villages of Islington, Hoxton and Shoreditch so enraged the citizens that fences were torn down. Ralph Agar's map of 1559 gives a picture of the Moorfield after this enclosing activity. There are laundresses stretching out clothes to dry on the tenter grounds, musketry and archery around the windmills, cattle and horses in the fields, and villas with gardens lining the lanes out of town.

In 1606, the Moor was raised, drained, laid out with tree-lined walks, effectively London's first park.

There is a Tenter Street behind Moorgate Station and the martial arts still practised in the grounds of the Honourable Artillery Company off the City Road, a space big enough for several rugby pitches. On part of the open land bought by the City for a burial ground, the non-conformists buried their famous dead on Bunhill Fields. Amongst those packed graves, bare trees and early flowers

26

are the prominent stones of Daniel Defoe and William Blake, side by side, both lovers of the countryside, one recording it in topographical detail, the other interpreting it in his own private visions of paradise.

Finsbury Circus came into the possession of the City Corporation in 1900, a simple oval of grass, including a bowling green, surrounded by plane trees and shrubs and a conspicuous display of spring flowers. The tulip tree planted for W.E. Cleary, who wrote about 'the flowering City', is thriving but the weeping ash is one of many trees that seems to be affected by disease. Though the City air is free from smoke, concentrations of sulphur dioxide are present and the emission from car exhausts may add to the pollution and affect the trees. The high temperatures and low humidity could produce physiological drought but most of the City's gardens are well tended and watered and the diseases affecting the trees are not fully understood.

Where Moorgate meets London Wall, there is a plaque on the wall of one of the towering office blocks that commemorates Sir Ebenezer Howard who was the founder of the Garden City movement. He lived in Fore Street, the street 'before' the Wall. His visions are still being maintained even in the overwhelming modernity of the Barbican redevelopment. Green lawns, flower beds, trees and water courses soften the severe architectural outlines. The centre piece is the Wall itself and its bastion of Cripplegate, the one place where the Wall alignment made a double dog-leg, presumably to avoid the marshy ground that would have made poor foundations for the stone structure. The Wall is fronted by a modern moat with a shoal of carp. Seen from the raised walkway they make golden patterns of movement. You can even hear them feeding as they rise to the surface.

The moat was frozen over in February 1978, with children skating on it just as their ancestors did in Norman times. The patches of reed-mace stood boldly out of the ice, their tall brown seed heads ready to break and scatter seeds like white fluff. The yard of Cripplegate church is another piazza, though early daffodils push through the gratings round the base of the trees. A small, secretive garden occupies the old churchyard of St Alphage, using the Wall as a sun-trap. The furry buds of magnolia are just unfolding, the yew full of male flowers ready to 'smoke' their pollen into the air and there, between them, at last, a young oak tree still holding its brown leaves, waiting with patience for Maytime and the warmth for a new leafing. North of the Wall the garden drops to a lower level filling the ditch that once fronted the wall. On the broken masonry, ragwort and other wild flowers find ample room for rooting.

Naturalists may have mixed feelings about the rebuilding of the Barbican for the bombed sites here were colonised by one of London's most unusual birds, the black redstart. About the size of a sparrow, the black redstart is so named because of its red tail. The rest of it is black with white flecks on the wing feathers. Mostly an insect eater, it was first recorded in London in 1926. London's wartime desolation gave it new territories, rough, unkempt corners where it could feed and breed in comparative peace. It became as much a symbol of the capacity of the natural world to bring life to the broken places as did the rosebay willowherb that became the common fire-weed of the bombed sites. One site, at Holborn, remained in its wartime plumage until 1977, but the rebuilding of London generally caused the black redstart to adjust yet again and now it is most frequently recorded in industrial premises such as power stations, gas-works and railway sidings. The recent atlas of London's breeding birds still shows it nesting in the vicinity of the City.

The Barbican looks like the hanging gardens of Babylon with its tier after tier of window-boxes. Window-boxes have been known in the City for at least five hundred years. Some of the brick-lined gardens at ground level are now sufficiently neglected for wild flowers to be ousting the planted ones. South of the Barbican there are enough small gardens to cause more than a minor diversion, such as one in Aldermanbury with Shakespeare's bust standing by a formal knot garden that could have come straight from Elizabethan England. The church of St Mary has been shipped off to Missouri, USA. Snowdrops, daffodils, camellias, broom, beech, yew, heathers and the trim topiary of box offer a varied floral surround for Shakespeare's two companions who published the first folio. Along Gresham Street, the sunken gardens of the Goldsmiths' Company join the churchyard of St Anne and St Agnes in another favourite lunch-time spot. There are poplar and fig and catalpa, acer and another oak tree. This sudden cheering assertion of the native scene is reinforced unexpectedly along Noble Street where the line of the Wall is still being cleared and, meanwhile, thistle, bracken and even coltsfoot are colonising. The coltsfoot is more conspicuous later in the year when the fat, fleshy leaves cover the ground but its flower, which appears before the leaves, may be seen breaking through the soil. There should always be some wild corners like this left to their own devices.

Across St Martin's Le Grand, there is yet another St Botolph's and yet another 'without', the third in the perambulation but this is the most important of the three, for this is one of the pioneer spaces laid out in 1880 in the grounds of no less than three churches. Known as Postmen's Park, it stands opposite the GPO in King Edward Street. To commemorate the first stamp to be issued with a tree on it, an oak tree was planted in 1973, quercus robur. Given another two hundred years or more, that oak may match the gnarled girth of the black poplar that leans by the path at the opposite end. This is the epitome of the City space. Surrounded by rather dull buildings, destined to long darkness, yet it is full of good things, chestnut, lime, plane, fig, camellias in flower, daffodils strewn over the banks. It has been a churchyard since pre-Norman times so that soil may have been tended for centuries. Like all the best spaces, it has its special features that make it memorable. Amongst the flower beds is a statue of the minotaur by Michael Ayrton and against one wall is the extraordinary memorial to Heroic Self Sacrifice founded by the Victorian artist, G.F. Watts, in 1887. Every enamel tile carries the story of someone who died trying to save others.

From St Botolph's church, the street called Little Britain leads up to West Smithfield, the great smooth field that stood at the north-west corner of the City, focus of droving roads, site of the slaughter houses and still the Central Meat Market. All the carcases are frozen now and the noise like heavy breathing comes from the refrigerators in the container trucks that wait for the market to open. Local street names like Cloth Fair and Hosier Lane indicate the trades that sprung up outside the west door of the priory church of St Bartholomew's. The narrow opening under the gatehouse leads to the most interesting and atmospheric church in London. The great nave has gone, replaced by a small churchyard, but the Norman chancel is bigger than many churches.

There is a mere green circle of grass, and trees with a frozen fountain, in the middle of the 'field', all that is left of the rallying ground for the peasant rebellion, the place where martyrs were burnt and the site of the great fair that survived until 1850. St Bartholomew's, Blackfriars, Charterhouse, Greyfriars, the Templars, the Knights of St John's all had their establishments nearby. All had their gardens, and their cloistered walks recalled now in small, green spaces, like Charterhouse Square. The best of the cloisters and courts lie beyond Ludgate to the west of the old City's walls and the river Fleet, in the Inns of Court that stretch from the Inner Temple by the river embankment north to Holborn and Gray's Inn. They give as great a sense of retreat and contemplation as any spaces in London. King's Bench Walk, Tanfield, Hare Court, Pump Court, Elm Court lead from one to the other like a medieval maze. I always aim for Fountain Court with its plane trees and gnarled mulberries leaning like Macbeth's witches over the fishes in the fountain pool, a winter sun-trap that opens out to the south by the emerald lawns and trim gardens of Garden Court sloping down to the Thames, spaces that have been tended for nearly a thousand years. The red and white roses recall the fateful choice for Yorkist and Lancastrian allegiance according to Holinshed's chronicles.

The Temple was famous for its rookery that Oliver Goldsmith observed, symbol in country lore of a fertile area. The rooks have proved less adaptable than crow or magpie and urban growth has driven their feeding grounds further away. The rooks were last recorded in 1916 and by 1947 the nearest rookery to Central London was at Lee Green, seven miles to the south east. Even that has been deserted now and the rooks have retreated to Eltham and to Wanstead.

A perambulation of the Inns is as rewarding as the walk round the City wall but is only possible on week days when the many ornate gates of wrought iron are open. Lincoln's Inn, north of The Temple, and Fleet Street, was once common land known as Fickett's Fields 'a common walking and sporting place for the clerks of the Chancery, apprentices, students of law and citizens of London'.[6] The field was tamed into a series of walks by commission of James I and planned by Inigo Jones. A royal proclamation of 1656 was needed to stop further encroachment of buildings.

The London County Council bought the private gardens in 1894 and opened them to the public giving us the pleasure of a large green with especially fine trees, as well as the architectural setting of one of London's best squares. Enormous plane trees, witchhazel in flower, snowdrops and daffodils are there, all the ingredients to entice the City workers at lunchtime to witness the waning of winter.

To the east, across Chancery Lane, lies Staple Inn with a small but lovely garden complete with the usual spring flowers and fine trees, including a fig. This was once the site of a wool staple and ancient fair held by Holborn Bars, the barred gateway to the City. This part of London is full of street names of 'gardens' and 'fields'. Few can match the elegance of Gray's Inn once a favourite resort of Samuel Pepys, and the almost rural elegance of Field Court and its massive iron pump. The private ground of the Inn holds some notable exotica, including a strawberry tree and a eucalyptus, easily recognisable even in winter.

When the Inns of Court leased these lands from the hospitals of St Giles and St John, they were pasture land. The dissolution of the monasteries led to a change of ownership and ultimately to redevelopment. In John Norden's map of London published in 1593, Gray's Inn is marked on the western limit of the built-up area, but London was about to grow dramatically. In John Evelyn's lifetime, the population of London doubled. Red Lion Square was laid out in 1698 and the countryside was in retreat from the City's walls. The village green, so to speak, was to be replaced by the city square.

3

ROYAL PARKS

In a small glade by hawthorn hedges and a patch of rough woodland, three rabbits grazed. Two pairs of mallard sat motionless on
the grass, heads tucked back. A squirrel scrambled down from a tree
and did a tumbling act with a fallen twig. A robin sang fiercely from
a branch of hazel fat with catkins. A magpie, a great tit and a linnet
emerged briefly from the woodland cover. The clearing ran down to
the water's edge where great-crested grebe were ducking and diving into the water for weeds and rotting leaves to place on their new
nest. Black-headed gulls were screaming above, their heads now
achieving the characteristic of their species. Coots chased each
other, heads down in angry show, paddling furiously across the
surface, one of them seeking retreat on the muddy bank. Beyond
this burst of spring-time aggression, the view lengthened into the
grassy distance and a stately avenue of trees focusing on to the
outlines of a country mansion to the west still misty in the early
morning sunlight. Only a distant stroller with dog impinged on the
image of a perfect March day in the countryside. Yet the setting was
near the centre of London, the country mansion was Kensington
Palace and the lake the Long Water in Hyde Park.

A hundred yards or so to the east lies another railed enclosure, a
bird sanctuary devoted to W.H. Hudson, connoisseur of London's
countryside. The first three birds I saw by the great bas-relief by
Jacob Epstein were bullfinches, greenfinches and a hedge sparrow
rustling amongst the thick undergrowth. Hudson admired the
thousand acres of green space in the West End but felt they were
mismanaged from the birds' point of view. He deplored the tidiness

of the scene and wanted more wild corners, with yew and holly, furze and bramble and native hedgerow plants to give the birds food and shelter. 'Make a spot in every park in London', he advised 'where the sedge warbler can breed'.[1] Hudson has had his way, sanctuaries have been enclosed and the sedge warbler is back in the royal park. Even a woodcock, bird of damp woods and boggy places, has been flushed from this very spot on a recent March day. Writing in the 1890s Hudson bemoaned the loss of the mistle thrush, the nuthatch, the spotted woodpecker and the increasing rarity of other species like the chaffinch, the greenfinch, the hedge sparrow and the spotted fly-catcher but according to the annual records of birdlife in the royal parks, all of those birds are back in residence except the woodpecker. In his time, even the magpie and jay were rare but now they can be heard chuckling in the innermost parts of the city. The birds are returning, their numbers growing every year. More than ninety species of birds are resident in Hyde Park now, at least thirty of them breeding successfully. Even the busy St James's Park can claim nearly eighty species, twenty or more breeding. The redpolls and herons are seen in Regent's Park and the kestrel and the long-tailed tit have returned and breed successfully. The trees and shrubberies of the parks attract wood-pigeons, tawny owls and carrion crows. The pinioned wildfowl and ducks on the lakes are augmented by winter visitors including rarities like the shoveller.

Some of the wild birds have become quite fearless and the Canada goose, migrant across the broad oceans, can be seen paddling along behind a family group as tame as a dog. One held up the traffic in the Mall, escorted by two red-faced policemen. Sanctuaries, water surfaces, cleaner air and the goodwill, not to say the abundant profferings, of visitors, make the parks a hospitable habitat for a great variety of birds and other fauna. This marvellous greenness of inner London, a chain of parks stretching four miles from Westminster to Holland Park, owes its origin to Henry VIII who, 'desirous to have the game of hares, partridge, pheasant and heron preserved in and about the honour of the Palace of Westminster, established a royal hunting ground stretching as far as Highgate and Hampstead, Islington and St Giles-in-the-Fields.[2] Deer were shot in this chase until the eighteenth-century and a herd remained in an enclosure on Buck Hill until the 1800s.

The hunting area stretched across the terraces of the Thames, well drained land with abundant springs, some of which supplied the Abbey of Westminster with a copious water source. Some of the wells can still be identified such as that devoted to St Govor, a sixth-century hermit, situated close to the Round Pond and crowned with a very unusual fountain that requires six circuits of its concrete to read the elaborate inscription. St Agnes's Well is now a loggia at the head of the Long Water and a plaque on the lower bridge over the lake mentions the spring granted to the Abbey, together with the Manor of Hyde, by Edward the Confessor. Henry VIII took possession of the land but his daughter, Elizabeth, confirmed the abbey's right to the water source. Two bourne streams flowed across the land, the Westbourne and the Tyburn, the former with its source in the heights of Hampstead to the north and its junction with the Thames at Ranelegh in Chelsea. These streams, dammed and diverted, became the serpentine lakes that are the central features of the parks.

Successive monarchs changed the landscape of the hunting ground in the fashion of their time and developed the royal road from the palace at Westminster to the palace at Kensington, the 'route du roi' which became corrupted to Rotten Row. That route became the first lighted way in the kingdom but was still dangerous enough in the eighteenth-century for footpads and highwaymen to ply their trade within sight of the seat of government. What better way to spend a March day than following that royal road through the countryside that lay to the west of London's second city?

The catalpas on the Embankment and in the courtyard of the Palace of Westminster are still bare and the long seed pods have fallen, to be brushed away, leaving the lawns trim and green.

The moat around the Jewel Tower to the south of St Peter's Abbey is a survivor of the many water courses that surrounded the royal settlement on the Isle of Thorney, a gravel site on the banks of the Thames. The moats not only supplied a defensive ditch and the harnessed power for the abbey mills, but also the fish ponds, an important part of the medieval diet. A fine carp selected from the abundant freshwater fish in the Jewel House moat caused the death of a fourteenth-century prior who choked to death when eating it. The food supplies for the abbey stood close by. The Domesday record tells us that the abbot of the monastery by St Peter's church held enough land in the village nearby to support eleven ploughs, nineteen villagers and forty-two cottagers with their gardens and woodland for one hundred pigs, grazing on the acorns and beech mast, the pannage of the forest floor. In the same area newly-planted vines were recorded by the patient scribes.

The farmland and the villages have gone from the scene but some memorable gardens remain, small enclosures even more serene and secretive than the City of London churchyards. Leave the bustle of the crowds round Parliament Square and walk past the Jewel Tower by way of Great College Street past ragstone walls which once lined the banks of the Tyburn, into the cloistered calm of Dean's Yard. The Home Farm stood here, now the playing field of Westminster School. The gateway in the corner leads into the Great Cloister and then by cool stone arcades into one of the city's remotest corners, the Little Cloister, ablaze with daffodils where the fruits of the fig tree are fat and green. Penetrating even further into the inner privacy of the abbey precincts the walks lead to the Abbey garden where poppies, dandelions, lilies, camomile and other herbs were cultivated, beehives kept and fish stews well stocked for Friday lunch. There were vines, too, providing a light, white wine. This garden, open to the public once a week, on Thursdays, is now a lawn large enough to contain two thousand people at a garden party. Some flower beds are maintained but the greatest pleasure in March is the walnut tree in full flower. One of the oldest gardens in England, tended for nine centuries, it gives us a direct physical link with the Domesday record as palpable as the Norman stonework of St Catherine's Chapel. Some of the catalpa trees in Westminster are amongst the finest in the country and, to maintain the tradition, another has been planted in Dean's Yard by the Worshipful Company of Gardeners, amongst the prevailing chestnuts.

It is difficult to drag yourself away from the peace of the abbey precincts but it is only a short step along Storey's Gate to the corner of St James's Park, to Duck Island and lawns erupting with crocuses ousting the snowdrops from our favour. Four pelicans are plodding in stately procession round the lake shore. Two cormorants dry their wings on a rocky islet. Canada geese sweep overhead, calling wildly. St James's established in 1532 lays claim to be the first royal park, for though Greenwich is older historically it was not royal when first enclosed. Charles II adored it, transforming its marshy meadows and ponds into a formal park with new avenues and a long canal, and setting aside an area to play pell-mell. George IV refashioned it again into a more informal landscape and restocked it with wildfowl, continuing the tradition started by James I. The park is nearly as famous for its birdmen as for its birds. I met one of them, an elderly man from Dartford, on an early March morning standing by the fig tree by the bridge. There were banks of daffodils round the trees, mallard sitting on the dry woodshavings in the rose beds, coots treading on the crocuses, three pigeons on top of a waste-paper basket by the willow which was just showing the first gentle green of new leaf. Then the birdman opened up the first of his plastic bags and the birds came screaming towards him. In two minutes I saw a greater variety of wildfowl and ducks than I had seen on the Kent marshes the previous week-end, getting cold and wet into the bargain. Shelduck, tufted duck, Canada geese, white-fronted geese, mute swans, black swan, pochards, black-headed gulls, pigeons, sparrows, blackbirds, coot and moorhen all arrived in quick, hungry succession. The sparrows came to hand, five on his hand at one time. The adult coots took the bread crumbs to their first brood and returned for more while the Canada goose chicks stole the first offerings. The black-headed gulls seemed to be winning in the general mêlée when along came the pelicans in full sail scattering all before them. The man from Dartford would not feed them. 'It would kill them,' he said. 'One died last year and we don't want that to happen again.' So the pelicans turned their attention to my brief case and plunged their mighty bills at me. I have seen these extraordinary birds leave the water and scatter the crowds on the path. They are the kings of the lake. Two recent additions have settled down well with the original four. When they drink the water sloshes around in their capacious bills. Many of the birds are pinioned but they are always joined by wild birds in the winter season and during migration. We can all be bird-watchers here with more than ninety species to absorb us with their antics. With such feeding fury all round, you have to admire the coot determinedly nesting amongst the branches of the great willows where they sweep down to the water. St James's was the site of the first introduction of tufted duck, white-flanked, black tuft on the back of the head, eyes like buttons. Now there are more than one hundred pairs there, though their breeding success is low. Competition for space is fierce and the mallard, commonest of the duck, have a mortality rate of more than

60 per cent, giving them an average life-span of little more than a year. The Canada geese, another introduced species, had their first successful brood in this park in 1926 and such has been the success of their adaptation that there are now more than two dozen pairs. Even the lesser black-backed gull and the herring gull have bred successfully, a rarity in London. On the whole, these inner parks can equal even the outer suburbs of the city in the number of their breeding birds. The density, that is to say the number of birds to an acre, is even higher, greater in fact than many woodlands and farmland. The willows, planes and other trees alongside John Nash's romantic lake are as good as you will find anywhere in London, drawing their ample nourishment from the water. Then we are distracted by the proud soldiers riding up the Mall, white plumes, scarlet cloaks, jet-black horses and we continue on our royal route past Buckingham Palace and its heather banks into Green Park, established by Charles II as a link between St James's and the wider spaces of Hyde Park.

Green Park is really green, essentially grass and scattered trees, but given visual variety by the rolling topography. The Tyburn once flowed through but the only sound of rushing water now is under a drain-hole cover. Notable are a beech hedge and a Lucombe oak, a hybrid which managed to retain a vestige of greenery throughout the winter. The strict line of the Queen's Walk, laid out by Caroline, George II's wife, so that they could 'divert themselves in the spring', leads to greater pleasures ahead.

Under the ferocious traffic of Hyde Park Corner the labyrinth leads to the wooded spaces of the old Manor of Hyde, where the sense of the open countryside is so palpable in the quieter days of winter that you would not be surprised if deer or fox crossed your path.

If St James's was London's answer to Versailles, Hyde Park is of the essence English. It has all the features of the landscaped garden established as early as the sixteenth century by such protagonists as Sir Francis Bacon who sought a three-fold balance between an inner garden, an extensive grassy area studded with trees and an area of wilderness. Hyde achieved them by accident rather than design. William III annexed a piece of the hunting chase to the west to create a Dutch-style setting for Kensington Palace. Queen Anne added some more and Queen Caroline would have taken the lot but the public enjoyment of the park was too well established to be so affronted. The result is a formal area with orangery, sunken garden, small lawns with clipped holly, bay and hawthorn lined up like soldiers, arbours and walled areas linked by broad avenues past the formal Round Pond to the more informal spaces east of the Serpentine. We can thank Caroline for the romantic sweep of the Serpentine, an innovatory conception that was to dominate most English parklands, breaking from the earlier tradition of long, straight waters such as that still in existence in Hampton Court Park.

The wilderness areas may be small but they are enough to break the great expanse of open grass and create a sense of diversity. They are even more important, as we have seen, for the encouragement of wild life, giving them sanctuaries for feeding and nesting that benefit the rest of the park. The birds make no such distinction of formal and informal landscapes and seem as happy splashing about in the privacy of the sunken garden, where the aconites are providing the first early colour, as they are in the fountains by Queen Anne's Alcove at the head of the Long Water or the public shores of the Round Pond.

Hyde does for the tree-spotter what St James's does for the bird-watcher. There are more than two hundred different species to identify though, admittedly, March is not the easiest time of the year for that particular exercise. But at least the visitor can enjoy the subtle variations of barks and branching formations and study the buds as they break into new life. Such close study will confirm the tragedy of the lost elms for the elm is one of the first trees to flower in the park, a flower of such delicacy and beauty that it will show a new splendour of trees quite as exciting as the spring flowers massed beneath them. Dark red flowers, clustered by the new shoots, give a reddish hue to the whole crown of the trees in March. The elm is one of the main trees of the royal avenues and its loss must be mourned as much for the loss of that glorious flower as for the fine tufty foliage of the tree itself. More than one hundred of them have been felled so far and more will follow. The buzz of the wood-saw here is a death knell rather than a pleasant recall of rural craft.

The other dominant trees of the avenues, chosen for their special qualities of shape, foliage and flower, include many introduced species, though the native oak and beech do make their appearance. The sweet chestnut is almost a native, having been introduced by the Romans. Easily raised from the nut, the tree may develop a fluted bark that looks like the carved columns of a Norman church nave. With fine foliage and crown, it is one of the longest living of the trees, achieving girths nearly as impressive as the venerable oak. The horse chestnut has its original home in Northern Greece and was brought to England possibly in the sixteenth-century and its popularity was spread by such admirers as John Tradescant of Lambeth. A modern admirer, Cyril Hart, describes the shoots flushing in March and the emergent foliage putting on 'the appearance of a damaged wing of a bird' showing that the tree has much visual delight to offer even before its flowering climax in May.[3] Horses do not like the nuts, though cattle may eat them. The word 'horse' if often used as an epithet for 'coarse', suggesting they are unfit for human consumption. The seeds have been used, though, to cure coughs in horses.

The lime tree may be a native but of the three hunded species, the common lime most frequently found in parks is a hybrid propagated from stock imported from Flanders, again in the seventeenth century, a time of great interest in trees, witness the enthusiasm of John Evelyn, author of *Sylvia*, admirer of avenues and formal gardens and most influential during the Restoration when the parks were being fashioned anew. The lime, together with the maple, is being used to infill many of the spaces left by the loss of the elms as in the Broad Walk at Kensington. By the palace, the trees are clipped and cosseted into unnatural shapes. In the open park, they are allowed to grow to their full natural stature. Along the Flower Walk south of the palace, they are planted in exotic conjunctions with shrubs and flowers, gingko, weeping beech, Californian laurel, cedar, magnolia, eucalyptus, flowering currant rubbing shoulders with cherry, yew and box like new fashions parading alongside the old reliables. The introduction of trees in royal parks had a great effect on their popularity and led to their adoption in many a private park and garden.

The trees matched the fashion of the people. Kensington was the superior end of the park where the stroller had to be dressed for the occasion.

> The dames of Britain oft in crowds repair
> To gravel walks and unpolluted air

Here, while the town in damp and darkness lies,
They breathe in sunshine and see azure skies.[4]

The skies are azure again after the Clean Air Acts of the 1950s and the air comparatively unpolluted. Six lichens are found in the heart of Hyde Park, a sure index of purity, as against the usual one or two in the City.

When Caroline was planning new gardens and promenading, Kensington was still a village to the west of London, the road from the park running through open country to Shepherd's Bush. Walking past the palace into Palace Green you still find a rural calm, almost a village atmosphere maintained by the approach through narrow lanes to the church of St Mary Abbot. The vision ends abruptly either in Kensington High Street or Notting Hill Gate but there is another fragment of the fashioned countryside a mile along that road to the west. Holland Park may not be royal in fact but it has a royal offering in the shape of the best piece of woodland left near the centre of London. The dense undergrowth, dominated by holly and bramble, makes it an even better cover for the smaller birds than the royal parks. Even the paths between the rustic railings are muddy, better for country brogues than town shoes.

The meandering track through the oaks and hawthorns leads into Lady Holland's Lime Tree Walk, the century-old trees so close that they make a natural canyon. Rhododendrons with fat, expectant buds, azaleas, holly, birch conceal the expected sparrows, starlings, blackbirds, jays, magpies, robins and chaffinches, then, in a clearing, you are suddenly confronted with unexpected peacocks, cranes and flamingoes shuffling through the woodland litter. The peacocks look more at home in the walled garden by the orangery, looking splendid on top of the brick wall, catching the sun. The cranes look more at ease alongside the yuccas and other exotica from the Japanese garden. A notable tree in this park, found especially on the terrace in front of the once-great house, is the holm oak, the ilex of the Mediterranean, with leaves like the holly, acorns like the oak and a bark like a tessellated pavement. The holm oak was another sixteenth-century introduction, just right in this architectural setting, showing all the magnificence of the erstwhile country house and garden.

The strange conjunction of flamingoes and oak woodland in

41

Holland Park is surpassed in the old hunting grounds of Marylebone. Rented out as farms, they finally became the visual climax of the Regency rebuilding of London's West End, the broad sweep of Regent Street and Portland Place penetrating beyond the built-up area to transform the northern farmlands into an even more elegant conception of royal landscape aspiration. Now in the early morning, you watch wolves and coyotes at their breakfast, herring gulls nesting on top of the Giraffe House and herons going through the involved panoply of nest building on top of the aviary. A magpie and a squirrel creep into the muntjac enclosure for the pickings. Regent's Park is strange countryside to evolve from London's eighteenth-century farmlands yet one that still witnesses one of the most traditional activities of the wild, the herons rebuilding their nests in the topmost branches of barren trees. Tudor monarchs hunted them, now they return to their sanctuary for the laborious start to the new season. Numbers once rose to more than sixty in the 1930s but the nesting pairs seldom exceed seven or eight at the moment.

Traditionally, herons return to the nests on St Valentine's Day and, in a recent hard winter, I walked through the park in sight of polar bears rolling in pleasure in light snow and found the lakes frozen, gulls and ducks slithering around on the ice but no signs of the herons. They were well hidden on their island home in the middle of the lake, all sitting, heads hunched into feathered shoulders, in the shelter of the trees. The rising temperatures of the March days brought them into the ritual activity, two on a nest, the male soaring down to the ground to select twigs, one at a time, to return after long, circular flight, and hand it over to the female which placed it with great deliberation on the nest. All the usual furore ensued when one heron occupied the wrong nest and another stole twigs from a neighbouring nest to save itself the greater effort of descent to the shoreline. Down there at ground level there were always the Canada geese to encounter, often charging the heron with heads down and challenging calls. There is only one larger heronry in the London area and that is on the reservoirs at Walthamstow in the Lea Valley where up to forty nests may be occupied. The herons of Regent's Park are the more remarkable for their sheer urbanity. I saw one of them once perched like a statue on the seat of a rowing boat, seemingly indifferent to the human activity all around. Beneath the heronry, a pair of great crested grebes are building their nest choosing wet leaves and mud and sodden weed rather than the herons' dry twigs. One dives. The other flies. Each bird to its own pattern. This is a marvellous time to observe the behaviour of birds, the trees bare, the views clear, the park quiet in the early morning. I encountered a university lecturer in the morning cold, watching the abundant coots with more than usual interest. He was reading the ring marks on their legs as part of his research. As they were slithering over thin ice of a late frost, the rings were easily observed. The bird sanctuary around the lake and its untouched wood and shrub layers make Regent's Park the most fruitful of the royal parks of inner London with nearly one hundred species observed. The bridge over the lake is nearly as busy with people throwing breadcrumbs as is St James's. The display boards help to identify the wildfowl and ducks, tufted duck and scaup, wigeon and shelduck, pochard, pintail, gadwall, pink-footed geese, white fronted geese, barnacle geese and many others. The yellow bill of the swan circling beneath announces a species different from the usual mutes. This area can also attract the first Spring migrants such as the chiffchaff.

Spring flowers and camellias open alongside the wildfowl, but the finest floral display is in the subtly contrived hummocks and ponds of Queen Mary's gardens, banks of crocuses under the leafing elder, snowdrops scattered under the weeping elm, daffodils by the fountain where icicles hang from long-haired nymphs. Moving north up the Broad Walk, the terraces of splendid mansions gleam in the sunlight and the sheep bleating in the children's zoo bring a sudden nostalgia for the open Downs and shepherds getting ready for lambing time. A stony clump of tree stumps, fossils from 150 million years ago, stand by holm oak and hawthorn, last reminders of the botanical gardens that were once as important as the zoological gardens here.

North of Regent's Park, across the Regent's Canal, lies Primrose Hill, technically an extension of the royal park. A very plain place with no primrose despite its south-facing slopes, it shows a bare scattering of trees, some pussy willow breaking into silvery buds. The hill is dull but the view is fine, encompassing all the royal hunting grounds that stretched from here to Westminster. There are trees enough amongst the urban silhouette to tease the imagination but the massive growth of the city is emphasised by the view to the north which is just as urban as the view to the south. An ancient sage, Mother Shipton, predicted that when London surrounded Primrose Hill, 'the streets would run with blood'. All looks very calm on this cold March morning, the nearest thing to a popular uprising being the kite-fliers on the windy hilltop itself. I choose the circuit to the west through the well-tended gardens of St John's Wood to the tube station which has so many palm trees in its forecourt that it looks like an oasis. Then back south to the greenery of St John's burial ground and the nursery end of Lords.

The East End did not see why the West End should have all the best parks. It needed the breathing space even more. 'A public park surrounded by good houses would attract wealthier residents, improve the tone and behaviour of the area', wrote an advocate of the time, putting very similar arguments to those used today for the creation of new parks in the most congested areas of inner London.[5] Perhaps more effective were the warnings that epidemics, once started, would not respect social boundaries and that the cholera and other diseases of the East End might affect the more fortunate areas of the west. The length of the working day and the working week did not allow the people of the East End to get into the countryside or the West End parks so the pressure grew for their own green space. An act was passed in 1840 'to enable Her Majesty's Commissioners of Woods and Forests to complete a contract for the sale of York House, and to purchase certain lands for a royal park'. The land chosen was an area where the artisans of London had once had the right to 'take and hunt hares, conies, foxes and other beasts' and in the course of doing so had resented early enclosures. But the enclosures for a new royal park met with local approval. The two hundred acres became Victoria Park, now on the boundary of Hackney and Tower Hamlets. Though it never became a royal park in fact, it received the royal seal, so to speak, when Queen Victoria visited the park on a bright, sunny spring morning in 1873, when the park was already well established, the planted trees and the flower gardens getting well into their stride. The centre piece of the park is a very large fountain, bearing the name of Angela Georgina Burdett Coutts, 1862, an impressive monument, almost a miniature Albert Memorial, that was to become the rallying point for East End dockers and other assemblies. The park now more than a century old and full of mature trees, has all the usual ingredients of the planned piece of countryside, avenues, tree clumps, a ring belt and exotica. Cedars, cypresses, a tree of heaven, tulip trees and holm oak stand amongst the native trees.

The concern for trees was more than just for their visual appeal and their effect as an antidote to the prevailing brick. Even in the lay-out of the Poors Land at Bethnal Green, it was stipulated that sixteen trees should be planted. The opinion was expressed that an oak tree evaporated eight times the rainfall and thereby helped to dry the soil and cool the air. So the trees of the East End would ameliorate the climate. The object of such parks and open spaces was the 'improvement of the General Health', a health that had been lost with the retreat of the countryside.

Created on the well drained gravels the hillocks had to be constructed from the material dug from the lakes. Hackney was once famous for the quality of its turnips and other market garden produce grown on disused gravel pits filled with city refuse. The gravels present problems to the park management giving a very hungry soil that needs constant attention. On the main lake is the usual competition for space between the ducks, the boats and the anglers making the most of the last days before the fishing season closes on the 15th of the month. On the far side of the lake, the banks are laden with shrubs and spring flowers. Two commendable practices that were established from the early inception of the park were the grazing of sheep to keep the grass down and the donation of surplus plants to the local people. Neither is carried out now but animals are not forgotten. There are enclosures for fallow deer with a good record of successful breeding, for chickens and rabbits, a great attraction for local children. The wildfowl on the lakes are nearly as varied as the West End parks and heron are often seen, flying in from their nesting sites in the Lea Valley.

To the north of the park lies a last fragment of Hackney's wildscape, Well Street Common, now suffering acutely from the loss of its elms. The path across the common leads through the nineteenth-century housing to part of South Hackney that has something of a village atmosphere with a church and a green and a pub. Like Regent's Park, Victoria Park has its canal skirting the southern perimeter, which is planned to become part of a long distance walkway along the tow-path linking the East End and West End.

Streatham Common 81

4

SPAS AND
COMMONS

As April opens the days lengthen, the warmth gathers and the trees reassert their floral authority. New leaf, new life. The fat buds of horse chestnut break and hawthorn opens alongside the early white blossoms of blackthorn. Bud scales and pollen gather in the cracks of pavements. Daffodils shake in the wind and showers make the parkland grass as green as fresh paint. Everything looks cleaner, brighter. People walk with a new spring in their step. Easter bonnets crown the parade in Battersea Park and the long, slim boats slide swiftly up the river by the crowded tow-path.

In other days, the inns of the Boroughs, on the south side of London Bridge, stirred with the feet of Chaucer's pilgrims ready for new horizons. The sights and smells of the countryside were close at hand in the wet meadows and marshes of St George's Fields flanking the Old Kent road. The timbered inns of the Borough still keep an old-world charm together with their country names, the hop factors' offices and the smells of fruit and vegetables from the market nearby.

For the less adventurous there were pilgrimages closer at hand, to the holy wells around the City. They were ancient in their fame. William Fitzstephen, writing nearly two centuries before Chaucer, recorded,

> There are also round London, on the northern side, in the
> suburbs, excellent springs, the water of which is sweet, clear
> and salubrious amongst which Holywell, Clerkenwell and St
> Clement's Well are of more note and most frequently visited,

as well by the scholars from the schools as by the youth of the city when they go out to take the air in the summer evenings.[1]

St Clement's Well stood to the north of the church in the Strand until 1874.

Between Clerkenwell and Islington is a mere mile, a very urban mile, joining the two 'village' greens. Between them are names that abound with memories of those salubrious waters, holy in the Middle Ages, much less so after their rediscovery in the seventeenth century. Nell Gwynn held court at Bagnigge Wells on the banks of the river Fleet and Sadler's Wells, once a holy well of St John's Priory, witnessed naval battles and river pageants to add diversion for the spa drinkers. In the same vicinity Chadwell was named after a Saxon saint. The area became the new Tunbridge Wells, visited by royalty and people of fashion, so much more convenient than the long haul into the Weald of Kent. The fashionable resorts were appalled by the audacity of this 'metropolitan mart of cakes, custard and stewed prunes'.[2] The wonders of water are not quite forgotten. A statue of Sir Hugh Myddleton, founder of London's modern water supply, stands on the corner of Islington Green, erected in 1862 when the green became a public open space. Opposite is the sadly-neglected facade of the Royal Agricultural Hall and more pubs with rural names like the Wheatsheaf. London's pubs are a constant link with country days. In the heart of a modern shopping centre you can imbibe a whiff of nostalgia with your ale under the sign of the Plough, the Jolly Farmers and the Black Bull. Only in the nineteenth century did the watering places become engulfed in the growing city. East of Islington Green, the heart of the old village has been transformed into a labyrinth of antique shops and markets. Somewhere at the back of the Royal Agricultural Hall, my father scrumped for apples in his Victorian boyhood. He showed me the place eighty years later with no difficulty in recognising the spot.

To recapture the sense of a trip to the wells and the open country now we have to follow the Fleet much further to its source five miles north of the City to the twin hills of Highgate and Hampstead. The springs that fed the river and made the hills famous come from the geological strata known as the Claygate Beds and the Bagshot Beds which overlie the London clay and form a natural reservoir. After the trim delights of the royal parks, we meet the wilder pleasures of the heath, the common and the oak woods, and clusters of houses and shops that bear the look of their country origins. Start at the foot of the hill by the high road or 'gate' out of town near Swiss Cottage underground station. There is a black cat by the roadside, curled in perpetual stone, eyes brightly looking back towards the south. An iron railing protects it. There the down-hearted Richard Whittington sat down on his way out of town, probably on the base of a wayside cross. There is another road-side stone near the top of Highgate Hill bearing the date, 1792, and initials indicating the boundary of the parish of St Pancras. Similar stones are found on Hampstead Heath. Highgate and Hampstead were waste-side hamlets with their medieval church and administrative centre south at St Pancras, a church that still stands in an island of greenery hard by the London railway termini.

Highgate 'village' is a series of interconnected spaces, the Grove, once possibly the site of the green, and Pond Square, still the venue for a modern spring festival, though no pond remains. Some of the best private gardens in the Grove, where Coleridge once lived, are open on April days to show their floral splendour. Finest of the private grounds is Waterlow Park, the gift of another Lord Mayor, a Victorian printer who presented the pleasure grounds of his mansion as a 'garden for the gardenless' in 1889. A large statue of the benefactor towers amongst the flower beds, backed by exotic trees. In a walled garden is an immense sun-dial recalling Andrew Marvell, the seventeenth-century poet who lived in a cottage nearby.

> How well the skilful Gardner drew
> Of flow'rs and herbes this Dial new

The park was fashioned from the woods that were once part of the Forest of Middlesex, haunt of robbers, wolves and boars and still, in the sixteenth century, the northern limit of Henry VIII's hunting area. A patch of that forest remains a mile to the north. After the exotica of Waterlow, the road-side avenues of lime, acacia, syca-more and holm oak, the seventy acres of Highgate Woods are as native as the oak. In some parts the oak is outnumbered by another native deciduous tree, the hornbeam, and the woodland enlivened with a mixture of birch, beech and rowan. This is one of many outer London spaces saved by the foresight of the Corporation of London, purchased at a time when they were endangered by speculative building. The wood has suffered the usual loss of flora and under-growth due to over-treading but recent attempts to encourage the regeneration of the trees have been made by fencing off some areas, together with some new planting, especially of oak. Another touch of imagination is shown in the building of alpine-type chalets on the edge of the open glades.

A more amenable wilderness for flora and smaller fauna lies below Waterlow park amongst the overgrown tombs of Highgate Cemetery. Between the ubiquitous daffodils is a proliferation of wild and cultivated flowers, lesser celandine, dandelion, ivy, colts-foot, the damp-loving horsetail with scilla, honesty and grape hyacinth. Such long-established and extensive cemeteries are amongst the best 'nature reserves' in London and are forming the basis of a new concept of park, the ecological park which some local authorities are developing. There is one in Newham Borough. Nunhead Cemetery, a forlorn jungle in South London, was regarded by W.H. Hudson as one of the best bird sanctuaries in London. It still is, for the colonisation by hawthorn, holly, elder and especially sycamore is rapid. Amongst the common or garden birds rustling around the tombs is the spotted fly catcher, operating from the top of a tall headstone in rapid forays for insects, always ready for flight to home base in an adjacent hawthorn.

From Highgate Wood by way of Highgate Village across to Kenwood and Hampstead Heath lies one of the best walks in the quest for London's countryside, linking fragments of one of its medieval hunting areas. The journey is three miles as the crow flies but this is an area that deserves a more meandering flight, a full day's perambulation. From Highgate Village, a public right-of-way leads down through the private opulence of Fitzroy Park, to the ponds of Highgate and Parliament Hill Fields. The boating pond is roaring with model boats and children playing and dogs swimming for sticks thrown by energetic owners but the adjacent pond is fenced off and allowed to develop a lush lakeside flora, shelter for coots, moorhen and mallard. The crowds watch two great crested grebes building their muddy heap of a nest by a willow in the centre of the pond. Spring migrants, a number of warblers amongst them, use this and other ponds for their summer residence. Such activity within the high-pitched buzz of model boats seems incongruous but the birds seem less disturbed than I do. A sequence of eight ponds leads upstream to the grounds of Kenwood. Above the ponds is Parliament Hill, its fields looking like pastoral intakes with straggly lines of hawthorns dividing up the hillside. They are little more than a century old and have a dramatic story to tell, another round in the long struggle for open spaces and one of the most important.

The protectors of Parliament Hill Fields were a group of far-sighted individuals who were determined to prevent the Lord of the Manor of Hampstead, Sir Spencer Maryon Wilson, from enclosing the common land. He claimed the right under the thirteenth-century Statute of Merton, to enclose the commons, to dig sand and gravel from it and then develop housing on it. He had lost one round in 1829 but he was a persistent man, refusing to make any concessions and new buildings appeared on the heath. Lord Eversley, with other supporters such as Robert Hunter (later to be associated with the foundation of the National Trust) formed the Commons Preservation Society in 1865. Hampstead Heath and Parliament Hill was to be the first major case for the new society to fight; the legal wrangles were to be bitter, costly and protracted. The death of Sir Spencer Maryon Wilson in 1868 eased the situation and his successors agreed to transfer his manorial rights to the Metropolitan Board of Works. 'It is especially important,' wrote Octavia Hill, one of those engaged in the battle, 'to keep the hill tops free from buildings so that the purity of the air blowing in from the country may be thus preserved.'

By the aid of a special committee set up for the purpose, the adjacent spaces were purchased, Parliament Hill Fields in 1889, Golders Hill in 1898 and the house and grounds of Kenwood in 1924. To such pioneers, their vision and persistence, we owe the survival of a square mile of open country made even larger in the imagination by the varied nature of the ground. More than 300,000 people visited it on a Victorian bank holiday and judging by the strollers, the kitefliers, the donkey riders, the footballers, the jog-trotters, the dog walkers and the Easter Fair it does not seem to have lessened in its appeal.

There is a tumulus, an ancient burial mound, on the summit in an enclosure of yew trees, a vantage point 'to beholde the statelie citie of London,' its gleaming tower office buildings and power stations rather than churches, but still a memorable viewpoint over the bricks and mortar and cement that might so easily have covered these green acres too.

Kenwood is the jewel, an eighteenth-century mansion in the Palladian style, designed by Robert Adam, with terraces, gardens, lawns, lake and trees. Hampstead is the heath, the wildscape. Yet the Heath is hardly a heath in the botanical sense since the cessation of common grazing, cutting of furze, lopping of branches and other traditional economies. There is little or no heather to be found. There are open areas with flowering gorse, birches and patches of bracken and sandy soils showing through the worn paths but, generally, the heath is reverting to woodland, the trees being more dominant than the spaces depicted in early prints and watercolours that can be seen in John Keats's house on the edge of the heath. Those prints show hay-making, cattle grazing, sportsmen shooting. John Constable and John Keats saw the Heath in its last entirely rural splendour.

The GLC Parks Department, has published a map of the Heath with suggested walks and useful annotations. A useful routine is to follow one of the many streams from its source, such as the iron-stone spring, on the West Heath that leads down to the ponds of Golders Hill. The west zones are less trodden than the dry heath and the flora is correspondingly more promising. Amongst the tall grasses is a forest of sycamore seedlings. On the Leg of Mutton pond, wrens and robins and dunnocks join the mallard and pair of whooper swans. Daffodils grow wild here and rosebay-willowherb emerges like a small red palm. I found one primrose and a cluster of wood anemones, the flower with the wind in its name that personifies the buffeting weather of early April. Most common of the wild flowers is the lesser celandine, growing abundantly even alongside well-trodden paths. Its name, according to Gerard, is derived from the Greek word for the swallow, and so called not because it flowers with the arrival of the migrant bird but because the 'dam' supposedly used it to restore sight to her young. Its yellow flower was also associated with butter and milk yields. It was cultivated as a medicinal herb, being used to assuage some unpleasant conditions of the abdomen.

A particularly good spot is the fenced enclosure by the pond in Golders Hill, squirrel, rabbit, great tits, blue tits, wrens amongst the cones and reeds, with a carpet of wood anemones. Then in the open park beyond an ancient boundary of hawthorn, yew and holly, the daffodils blaze in subtly contrived informality in the old orchard, preparation as it were for the appearance of cranes and peacocks, deer, wildfowl, and flamingoes, the little zoo that teaches London children so much more about exotic species than it does about the native animals. A London child will recognise Jacob's sheep before it knows a Southdown, a water deer before a Friesian cow.

The northern extension of the heath repeats the pattern of Parliament Hill with hedgerows of hawthorn with some colonisation by elder, holly, oak, hornbeam and a rare blackthorn, dividing up the wet fields on the London clay, but not wet enough to deter the footballers. One of the keepers told me that the springs breaking out from the gravel cap of the Heath are so copious that sheet water fed by heavy rain once swept sand all over the grass and over the boundary roads into adjacent gardens.

The initial cause of Hampstead's popularity lies in a quiet lane to the south of the Heath in Well Walk. By a raised pavement stands the recently restored well, erected to the memory of the third Earl of Gainsborough who first granted the well and six acres of land to the poor of Hampstead in 1698. John Constable's house in Well Walk is marked by a plaque. This is the heart of Hampstead 'village', the area now under a conservation order, clustered round the spire of Christchurch. Most famous of its buildings is the house of John Keats, now library and museum, where he listened to the nightingale.

The nightingale is not amongst the present resident birds although more than fifty breeding species are now recorded, including such spring migrants as the chiffchaff, the willow-warbler, the garden warbler, the whitethroat, martin, swift and cuckoo. This is twice the number of breeding species to be found in the inner parks such as Hyde Park and equal to such a rural vastness as Richmond, a tribute not only to the varied habitats of the Heath but also to the large private gardens, the golf courses and grounds of large institutions around the Heath. There are many secretive corners where the birds can find cover. Richard Mabey, chronicler of London's 'unofficial countryside', recounts how he got lost in such a corner of the Heath but was much rewarded in finding such botanical pleasures as amphibious bistort, marsh pennywort and Himalayan balsam on a summer's day. The summer flora is more varied than that of the early April days but at any season the Heath can only offer a pale shadow of the botanical richness that existed when it was used as a training ground by the Society of Apothecaries, collecting their culinary and medicinal herbs.

The symmetry of the London basin produces the mirror image of Hampstead, on the south side of the river at Dulwich and Sydenham. Hampstead is the higher of the two hill ridges, 134 metres compared with 109 metres at Crystal Palace. Both are equidistant from the city centre. Crystal Palace too, lies on a capping of Claygate Beds overlying the London clay. The boundary stones of St Pancras have their counterpart in the metal posts on Honor Oak marking the boundary of Camberwell. The gravel cappings are residuals of a deposit that once covered much larger areas before being eroded by London's rivers. Geologists include them in the Eocene rocks, the deposits that mark the dawn of the current conditions of geological creation, fifty million years old.

The search for the healthy life by way of spa waters, clean country air and the promenade has found its modern expression in the Crystal Palace sports centre with running tracks, swimming baths, playgrounds and leafy training areas set out on what were once the verdant slopes of Penge Common before its enclosure in the nineteenth century. The transfer of the Crystal Palace to Penge Common excited Joseph Paxton, fresh from Chatsworth, to produce plans that would 'throw Versailles into insignificance'. All that is left of that dream are some neglected terraces with sphinxes and a statue of Dante gazing over the outer suburbs of South London. The rest is sport. Some century-old surprises lurk around the lake in the lower reaches of the parkland. Eight coots fight beak and talon to establish territories around the massive frame of a plesiosaurus. A megalosaurus towers above flowering gorse and the iguanodon, which reputedly housed the opening ceremonial dinner in 1854, stands toe-deep in daffodils.

John Ruskin did not like the Crystal Palace 'for ever spoiling the view'.[3] From his new home in Herne Hill he often walked the wooded ridge that 'rose with the promise of all the rustic loveliness of Surrey and Kent'. With the Palace came the railways and roughs who roared at the cows and tore down the blossom of the trees. Yet the great Victorian urged his readers to remember that their rights of way were amongst the ancient and cherished of common rights.

One of his companions on his rural rambles was the young Octavia Hill who shared his enthusiasm for the open spaces and devoted her later life to their protection.

Penge Common was only one part of an extensive area of woodland and heath and common that was known variously as the Northwood (of Surrey) and the Westwood (of Lewisham). Woodland names abound in the area today, Norwood, Westwood Hill, Forest Hill, Honor Oak, One Tree Hill, Gipsy Hill. The gypsies camped by the wells in the days when John Evelyn travelled out from Deptford and even King George III came along to try the remedy, protected by his Life Guards. Springs broke out all round the hills, Dulwich, Sydenham, Streatham and at a later date, Beulah developing as minor spas, some like Beulah remaining fashionable until the nineteenth century when the seaside took the trade away and they became residential areas. Only in the last two decades have the detached Victorian villas standing in extensive grounds given way to modern block of flats and close-packed town houses. One of the most famous group of wells at Sydenham was on the site of what is now Wells Park, opened on Whit Monday, 1901, a place of willows and water so formal and contrived that the sight of flamingoes amongst the wildfowl seems quite natural. The altar of the Victorian chapel reputedly stands on the site of one of the twelve wells. Another story insists that the water had been used to recreate the varied sections of the Rhine, the area having been a favourite residence for German business men. A visually delightful park, it retained some hornbeams and blackthorn that are much older than the formal park and recall the ancient wood that straddled the hills.

John Aubrey, the Surrey antiquarian, recalled 'the great wood called Northwood belonging to the Archbishop of Canterbury wherein was anciently a tree called the Vicar's Oak where four parishes met.'[4] At the time he was writing, the great wood had been decimated by the Cromwellians, leaving only nine thousand oak pollards and ninety timber trees where Charles I had hunted. With its despoilation came the Croydon Colliers cutting the trees to supply charcoal for the London bakeries. Attempts to enclose the common in the seventeenth century by James I met with prolonged and successful local resistance led by the Lewisham parish priest, Abraham Colfe, with the illegal fences torn down and a deputation to the king. The nineteenth century enclosure was apparently

unopposed, Norwood Common in 1808, Dulwich in 1805, Westwood in 1812 and Penge in 1827. There is a small patch of woodland
on the very summit of One Tree Hill, sixteen acres saved by the
Camberwell Parish Council, 'for the use of the public for ever' in
1924, mercifully unkempt and left to the native deciduous trees.

The best circuit of the ancient wood starts from Dulwich Wood-
house and follows a track, Lower Cross Lane, down through the oak
woods of Dulwich, a private woodland, fenced in but easily
observed from the path. Its privacy and its variety make it a favourite spot for bird-watchers. I met an enthusiast on a sunny Sunday
who was delighted with the first seasonal sighting of the blackcap,
the chiffchaff and the willow warbler. Amongst the abundant greenfinches and goldfinches he had seen a wheatear which was pausing
awhile on its migration from the warm south to wilder northern
horizons. His real 'patch' was Elmers End where he had seen sedge
warblers nesting. He knew his ornithological London well, had seen
black redstarts in Surrey Docks and heard one singing by Broad
Street station. He reminded me of Richard Jefferies, the naturalist
and author who had lived for a time at Sydenham nearby. Jefferies
could see little beautiful in the place but had commented that 'the
birds care nothing for appropriate surroundings.' These green oases
of suburbia are even more 'appropriate' for variety of birds than
many outer rural areas.

The hill ridge, like that of Hampstead, forms a boundary zone
for many breeding birds, such as the tree-creeper, the linnet, the
goldcrest, the redpoll and the warblers. They are much more likely
to be observed outside that five mile radius than within it. The total
number of breeding species, about fifty-six in recent years, is almost
identical with the heaths and woods of Hampstead. The chance of
seeing rarer spring migrants is increased, too.

I shall never forget a Sunday afternoon when the family were
watching the usual consort of sparrows, starlings, blackbirds and
thrushes alighting on our lunch-time offerings, when a small
scarlet-crested bird appeared, fed briefly and left us in wonderment.
I identified the visitor later in an aviary in Battersea Park as the
cardinal bird from South America. Migrant, vagrant or escapee from
a private collection, it left us hoping for a repeat appearance
throughout those April days.

At the bottom of the path through Dulwich Woods, the road

leads right to a toll-gate, a rare but cherished anachronism, past playing fields divided by hawthorn hedgerows that date from the enclosure of the common. The best of them, with holly and elder invading, sycamore saplings thriving in their shelter, lie up a private cul-de-sac called Grange Lane. Past the toll-gate towards Dulwich Village, the old brick and clap-boardings of Ponds cottages confront the Victorian gothic of the famous College. Then wooden signposts and old roadside stones that mark five miles to the Treasury at Whitehall announce entry to the village, and a selection of architecture that covers nearly three centuries, from impressive eighteenth-century villas to one cottage that has a frontage of just two paces.

Dulwich is memorable for its trees. Those along the village street include a lovely line of tulip trees. A small, but unusual collection stands in the trim lawn of the art gallery and in Dulwich Park, according to the notes on the tree-trail by the GLC Parks department, there are at least thirty-two different species from the oak to the Kentucky coffee tree. Scattered between the usual ponds, gardens, aviary and lawns are some really big pedunculate oaks, quercus robur, in all their glory. The park was created in 1885 from five fields of Court Farm, a late compensation for the loss of the Common earlier in this century, but the oaks are much older, their alignment suggesting centuries-old boundaries. The display of daffodils and crocuses beneath their rugged boughs is a feature of April in the park, one of the best of its genre in London.

The path through Dulwich Park leads uphill to Lordship Lane as it climbs up the forest ridge. The road-walk is worth the effort, if only to reach Horniman's Museum and its surrounding park. There on Surrey Mount, in 1859, Mr Horniman, tea merchant, collector and philanthropist, set out his estate and grounds. Now owned by the Inner London Education Authority, the grounds are used as nature trails. By far the most interesting is the nature reserve along the disused railway line that bounds the park to the west. The judicious planting of trees and flowers among the scrubland that has developed along this well-drained site adds rather than detracts from its botanical interest, a very imaginative project that deserves copying. Horniman's can also boast a small zoo with an eccentric conjunction of barnacle geese and wallabies alongside an oak.

John Rocque's map of 1762 not only shows the great North

Wood as being the largest area of woodland within five miles of the City but also tongues of more open common land running from it towards the villages clustered round it, such as the Rye leading to Peckham and the long common of Streatham. Peckham Rye, for the most part a rather dull grassy triangle, had an eventful history, gaining notoriety due to its huge fair. On one occasion many wild beasts belonging to Mr Wombwell 'took possession' according to contemporary accounts. The Lord of the Manor wanted to stop such activities, and enclose much of the Rye, but the local people resisted and by 1882 it was saved as a public open space. The fine park to the north was added from farmland. Part of this garden created round one of the many spring-fed streams from the wooded hills is named after J.J. Sexby, nineteen years the chief officer of London's parks in the heyday of their inception and author of the finest book about them.

Most famous of the South London spas was at Streatham on the western edge of the North Wood. You could still sample the mineral waters in the 1920s, in a small house behind a dairy in Valley Road, the last survivor of London's abundant watering places. Streatham water was supplied to London coffee houses and hospitals. Dr Johnson was a frequent visitor with his friends, the Thrales, who lived nearby. Everyone drank Streatham water. The common became a fashionable promenade. The present high street is a place to be hurried through, following the line of the Roman road to the south, but Streatham deserves a longer stay. The common stretches from the busy main road up the long, grassy slope to the wooded hill-top. Almost hidden in a dell by that woodland is the site of an earlier spa discovered in 1660 by labourers when their horses stuck in a quagmire. The water that made the mire also made Streatham. John Aubrey, who visited the place soon after its discovery, declared that three cups of Streatham water equalled nine from Epsom. A well house was erected and pleasure grounds laid out. Now called the Rookery, those grounds are still there for our pleasure, enclosing a well-head in a walled garden. The place is a sun trap with a panoramic view to the south and west, framed by cedars, a magnolia breaking into beauty and a foreground of green fields that makes the rooftops in the distance seem an impertinence. One of the walled enclosures is devoted to white flowers in all seasons, a heavenly place on a quiet day.

From the Rookery, a track leads along the woodland edge to Norwood Lodge that was once the site of Charles II's hunting lodge, as good a place as the last vestiges of the great North Wood of Surrey can offer to sit in the spring sun and watch the season unfold.

5

GREENWOOD

The May Queen, dressed in buttercup yellow and Dutch bonnet, surrounded by her retainers carrying arbours, bouquets and tulips, walked in proud procession down the hill, the Scout band leading, drums setting a brave marching rhythm. Behind them came the Brownies and the Cubs and the toddlers in fancy dress turning the High Street into a ribbon of gaiety. After a cheerless, cloud-laden morning, the sun relented and broke through just as the procession reached the corner of the common, where the maypole stood ready. The dignitaries made their brief pronouncements and the Queen was crowned. Then the maidens danced their well-rehearsed labyrinth of steps and the bright ribbons twined and untwined round the maypole, symbol of the greenwood. Chislehurst was celebrating the renewal of the floral kingdom as it has for more than half a century, one of many London 'villages' that has restored ancient customs.

The greenwood was tardy in its greetings. By tradition, the May revellers went into the woods to gather garlands especially of the may flower but the hawthorn on the common had barely been in leaf for a week or so and the blossom would not be out until May was well on its way.

In the church of St Nicholas, a fine medieval church of flint and ragstone, which stands on the south side of the extensive common, there may be a tangible connection with an earlier spirit of May Day. In the Scadbury chapel, amongst the fine memorials of the local families, the Sydneys and the Walsinghams, there is under a corbel a small carving of a face with wide eyes and bulging cheeks. The local histories dismiss this carving as a grotesque, possibly of late Norman craftsmanship. On close inspection, one of the cheeks at least still shows the stem and outline of a leaf, a typical Jack-in-the-Green, one of the essential characters in the medieval May Day revels, spirit of the earth's renewal with foliage curling from his mouth.

Recorded long before Domesday, the church can boast a small Saxon window. Chislehurst still lives up to its Saxon name, the stony place in the forest, with the wooded common as its central feature and the village really a cluster of hamlets standing in small clearings round its perimeter. On the common is the broad bowl of a cockpit and a pound where livestock were kept. The place can claim at least two royal connections for the first Queen Elizabeth graces the village sign, knighting Francis Walsingham and, on the common, an enormous memorial commemorates the death of the prince imperial, son of Napoleon III who chose this Kentish village for his exile.

> In the month of May, namely on May Day in the morning,
> every man except impediment would walk into the sweet
> meadows and green woods there to rejoice their spirits with
> the beauty and savour of sweet flowers and with the harmony
> of birds, praising God in their kind.[1]

The people of Chislehurst can still follow John Stow's injunction written nearly four centuries ago for Hawkwood Lane leads from the church down into farmland with cattle grazing and beyond into Petts Wood, now in the possession of the National Trust. The wood purchased by public subscription in 1927 in memory of William Willett, 'untiring advocate of Summer Time', is heavily used with wide well-trodden paths but in the damper corners under the alders by the railway embankment there are a handful of flowers to welcome May, celandine, violet, coltsfoot, creeping buttercup, wood spurge and the first bluebells, a poor offering for a Tudor reveller but as good as our much used spaces can offer on the first day of May.

Such celebrations were once held in the heart of the City. There is still a maypole strapped to the walls of an office building by Shaft Stairs near the church of St Andrew Undershaft, so named because it stood by the 'shaft' of a maypole in Leadenhall Street. In those days the City fathers needed to ride no further than the woods of

Stepney, just beyond the Tower, to gather their floral tributes.

On a May day, King Henry VIII rode with his Queen Katherine, with many lords and ladies, to the high ground of Shooters Hill, four miles through open country from his palace at Greenwich. There they met two hundred tall yeomen, all clad in green, led by one Robin Hood. In the oak woods on the hill, the merry men shot arrows to the great delight of the king. 'Robin Hood', continues John Stow, the chronicler of this royal occasion, 'desired the king and queen, with their retinue, to enter the green wood where, in harbours made of boughs, and decked with flowers, they were set and served plentifully with venison and wine'.[2] Whether this was an elaborate masque or a reflection of the wildness of the fringes of Kent, it offers just the right incentive for us to follow in the royal footsteps, or should it be, hoof-prints, and see what remains of that sylvan scene, what pleasures for a modern a-maying.

There are inn-signs of the Green Man in the district, perhaps a reference to Robin who sought a precarious sanctuary in the surviving greenwood or, more likely, to Jack-in-the-Green. There are royal palaces and oak woods, may blossom and deer still to be seen on the way. We have our celebrations, too, though not of venison and wine. At the centre of a crowd down by the Cutty Sark, at Greenwich, the Morris men are leaping and banging sticks, bells ringing, music playing, drinking copiously between their exertions in the true tradition.

Henry set out from his palace of Placentia. The foundations were discovered by excavations in 1970, beneath the lawns of the Royal Naval College. We barely had time to admire them and visualise another Hampton before they were covered over again. A house on the north side of Greenwich Park lays good claim, judging by its brickwork, to be part of Henry's tilt-yard. That apart, the only certain survivor of Henry's Greenwich is a massive, hollow hulk of an oak tree, now fenced in. It officially died in the last century but the prolific ivy and the numerous birds that nest in it make the trunk a very lively skeleton. The Elizabethan oak inevitably attracts its legends, that Henry and Anne Bullen danced round it with the baby Elizabeth resting in it (it must have been ancient even then). It also claims to have been a lock-up for malefactors in the park.

The park was enclosed by a wall by James I in 1619. Much of James's brick wall survives but the landscape within it now has little to do with the Tudor hunting park. For the restored Charles II turned Greenwich into a new exercise in formality and grandeur to rival those of the great continental parks he had seen during his exile. John Evelyn, with his estates at nearby Deptford, was a friend of the King, a lover of trees and an ardent advocate of the new 'avenues' and other continental devices. The advice of a famous French gardener, Le Notre, was sought and the avenues of elm, chestnut, and limes and oak made geometric patterns across the old hunting ground. The steep escarpment, an old river cliff of the Thames, in the middle of the park broke the visual effect of the pattern just as it focussed on the magnificent architectural group being created on the site of Placentia. Much has happened since to modify the pattern and the present intention is to restore, as much as possible, the initial concept, including the flights of terraces that led from the cliff top where General Wolfe's statue now stands, towards the Queen's House. The Dutch elm disease has decimated the avenues and removed one of the favourite Carolingian trees. I counted the rings of several old elms as they were felled and found them to be just over three hundred years old, dating back to the very years when Charles planned the new landscape. Nevertheless, many new trees have been planted to fill in the spaces, notably beech, hornbeam, lime, Turkey oak and horse chestnut. The infinite variations of new greenery refresh the eye at every turn but the flowering of the horse chestnuts is the final coup d'oeil. The Eltham Walk, now called the Blackheath Avenue, cannot match the mile-long avenue of Bushy Park for sheer grandeur but it is as royal in its aspirations.

On either side of the Eltham Walk were two areas known as the Little and the Great Wilderness. The Little Wilderness is now a cricket ground, one of the loveliest in London but the Great Wilderness has been enclosed and planted with exotic trees and flower beds and a duck-filled pond surrounded by willows and magnolias, heathers and azaleas. The loss of the wild area is easier to accept when confronted with such marvellous conjunctions of colour and shape, dwarf palms and bluebells by the Spanish gorse, tulips by the deodar cedar. Behind a high fence amongst the oak trees, are the last of the deer that once roamed free throughout the park. Only about twenty of the fallow herd are kept, but, recently, a red stag with six does has been brought from Richmond. The stock may have links with the deer of the original chase but many of the royal parks were restocked by James I, bringing in fallow deer from Norway.

The deer are confined but the squirrels run free, much to the delight of the children but not for the forester. The damage they do to buds and growing shoots of young trees and to barks is great. Yet they are so important as a touch of the wild in this urbane area that their loss would be felt. I say wild, but some of the squirrels have become almost tame. They will not only approach for tit bits but even leap on laps and shoulders of the unwary with piratic gait and the shabbiness of a highwayman. I have watched one methodically clearing up the area by the café, inspecting every crumb for comfort and finally licking a choc-ice wrapper with fastidious care.

The grey squirrel is not a native of the greenwood. Henry would not have seen it. It was introduced in the late nineteenth century and spread rapidly, ousting the red squirrel from its traditional woodland territories. The abundance of acorns and beech mast and pine cones was much to its liking. In Greenwich, the squirrels' diet is varied with every imaginable tit-bit from the passers by. The adaptation of the squirrel reached its climax for me when I saw three of them by the café on Shooters Hill, under the shadow of the castle of Severn Droog, loping out of the woodland and accepting three ice cream cornets. On that occasion they sat in a row and finished the ices off. I thought I was in a circus.

The birds are not forgotten at Greenwich. The small pond choked with ducks is the main attraction. Mallard, tufted duck, pochard, ruddy shelduck and that most improbable of all the ornamental fowl, the mandarin duck, gabble round to accept the abundant offerings. But many of the regulars give their attention to the common or garden birds that are busier than ever in the nesting season. The sparrows and blue tits line up along the railings for their bread and cake, joined by an occasional blackcap and greenfinch. Even the spotted flycatcher has its regular patch not far from the Elizabeth oak while that venerable hulk is always groaning with birds, sparrows, blue tits, pigeons, crows, starlings and finches. There are no less than forty sparrows nesting in one tree in the park. The density of birds is nearly as high as in a rural park. Altogether no less than seventy different species of birds were recorded at the last annual count, at least twenty-six of them breeding there, including the goldfinch, the wren and the tawny owl.

Just beyond the park gates lies the open common of Blackheath. Once it was covered with pastures, wood, heath and gorses, the wasteland of the surrounding manors. Now it is flat and rather dull, stained with patches of sheep's sorrel, grassy levels for sportsmen. There is little to frighten the traveller, few hiding places, gorse-laden, heather-shrouded hollows that gave the highwaymen their cover. A few pits remain in the north-west corner where gravel was extracted for ballast, but not a sign of the windmills that graced the early topographical sketches. Just one isolated mound covered in birch and gorse breaks the line, perhaps a tumulus, perhaps the mound where Whitfield preached. But the heath has its memories of glory and great events, the great mustering ground on the highway from the coast to the capital. There the 100,000 peasants gathered, led by Wat Tyler and Jack Straw. There Jack Cade mustered his rebels. More peacefully, the citizens went to greet Henry V from triumph at Agincourt. Henry VIII transformed it into a cloth of gold amongst the golden gorse to greet Anne of Cleves and George III reviewed his troops in another Maytime. The gorse was often burnt, by accident or design, in the great celebrations. This is one of the many heaths that has been linked with the opt-repeated story of Carl Linnaeus, the famous Swedish botanist, who fell to his knees and thanked God for the beauty of gorse in bloom. When he visited London, he landed at Redriffe, close by, so the claim has some foundation.

The enclosure of Greenwich Park was the first of the incursions on the heath. From the seventeenth century onwards, the houses, gardens and estates of the rising gentry nibbled at the edges of the heath, stealing the common land but, at the same time, giving the area now some of the most interesting architecture in London, spanning four centuries. There are still boundary stones and metal pillars scattered across the heath that show this was London's boundary as recently as the 1880s when the new London County was created. In my father's boyhood, the open country began here with footpaths and fields leading south-east to rural Kent. As the tide of housing has swept on, much of the common land of Lewisham, Charlton, Woolwich and Eltham has been left open, a reminder of the medieval landscape and the notorious road in the path of the Romans over the summit of Shooters Hill and its dense oak woodland.

Blackheath still has its regular fairs and in recent years a May festival has been instituted, a much less lawless affair than those that gave the heath its black reputation, and made John Evelyn wonder what good purpose such a fair served so close to London. The army stands by with professional nonchalance by guns and helicopters while Marines do daring things on motorbikes and, in the late evening, a man dives off the top of a tower, blazing with fire, into a water tank. Youths chaff and shout and a little girl goes up to kiss him, recognising a truly heroic figure in a mundane age. He wore a top hat with his swimming costume.

Charlton, the next township to the east, is not so fashionable but has more claim to the name of 'village' than Blackheath which was really a commonside hamlet, the medieval parish centre being at Lewisham. Charlton's main street is called 'the village' and the manor house, one of the finest seventeenth-century buildings in London stands to one side. The church lies opposite. Between the two main buildings was the village green, later annexed to make a more imposing entry to the manor house. By its side stands a mulberry tree with a plaque that claims it to be the first planted in England in 1608 by order of James I who sought the revival of the silk industry. He also brought golf with him from Scotland and the Royal Blackheath Golf Club claims to be the oldest in the country. The pleasure grounds behind the manor house have walled gardens and a fine display of trees, avenues, and groves of holm oak and yews, separated by a ha-ha ditch from the park beyond where the deer, depicted in early prints, were kept.

The commons and woods of Charlton remain only in fragments. The manorial lords, the Spencer Maryon Wilson family, were amongst the most active developers of their estates, holding firmly to their manorial rights to enclose the commons. While Blackheath was transferred to public ownership by the Dartmouths in 1872, Charlton's spaces were less fortunate. The Horn Fair, presumably named after the products of horn sold there, gained a bad reputation. 'A village,' said Evelyn, 'famous, or rather, infamous, for the yearly collected rabble of mad people, at Horn Fair.'[3] It has been revived in recent years, more sedately, with Morris dancers and other medieval accoutrements. The local inn sports the sign of a hunting horn. The hanger woods of Charlton were added to the local amenities as recently as the 1920s. On its northern edge is the sand quarry famous for its fossils that once fed sand to the local glass-works and gun-mouldings of Woolwich. The chalk is not far from the surface here and the flora of the less trampled corners has many pleasant surprises such as alkanet and herb Robert. In the well-wooded lower park are small enclosures of fallow deer, Jacob's sheep, goats, ponies and rabbits to delight the local children.

Most of Charlton's common went the same way as that of Woolwich, taken by the military during the Napoleonic wars. It's more like an enormous parade ground than a common but the grassy waste is surrounded by a hawthorn hedgerow full of fine May flower. Even on this dull waste I counted more than twenty-two wild flowers in bloom, including a show of bluebells amongst long coarse grasses. Mallow, shepherd's purse, white and dead nettle, stinging nettle, ragwort, cow parsley, dandelion, sheep sorrel, plantain, chickweed, groundsel, Yorkshire fog, rye grass, these are the urban plants that survive treading, mature quickly, throw their seeds by the thousand, and find lodgings in cracks of pavements and road-side wastes. There are other floral survivors, too, in those curious little nature reserves, the ha-ha ditches that look more like tank-traps in this setting than a landscape gardener's surprising ploy. Beyond the ditch lies the Artillery barracks, one of the finest Georgian façades in the country, a thousand feet of architectural splendour and, in the grounds, the typical trees of the period, white poplar, whitebeam, holm oak making strange visual conjunctions with Crimean cannons and other hardware. In recent years, new trees have been planted on the common to add a much-needed touch to its visual amenity.

The hawthorn-lined bounds of Woolwich Common point directly to Shooters Hill. The road, hemmed in by woodland, was not widened until 1733 and then the subjugation of Robin Hood's hunting tract began in earnest. A stone mounting block still stands by the roadside at the summit, the highest hill in inner London. One of the first buildings to be erected was a folly castle called Severn Droog, built in 1784 to commemorate a battle on the far-off Malabar coast. Before that, the gibbet had been the most conspicuous landmark. The cut-throats' paradise became the healthy playground of the newly-rich, an ideal rural setting for new villas. The first major incursion into the oak forest came with the development of Shrewsbury Park in 1789, a large estate with mansion near the summit of the hill and extensive grounds round it. When the estate broke up in this century, the mansion became a community centre and much of the ground was built on but the spaces that survive with names like Eaglesfield are studded with good trees and command panoramic views over the Thames. Even within the present roads, several trees of great age and girth have been preserved. Other smaller houses followed, Castle House in 1823, then Jackwood, eventual home of the Beerbohms. This rural retreat, so near London, with its woods and fields and views became a favourite haunt for the theatrical profession and it is said that Edward, the Prince of Wales, walked with Maxine Elliott, the actress, on the terraced gardens that remain there.

Shooters Hill, too, has achieved the visual balance of the classic English parkland, a formal pleasure ground, a park with lawns and occasional trees, surrounded by the wild woods. The various parcels of land, Oxleas, Jackwood, Castlewood, Eltham Common all came into the hands of the London County Council in 1922 as a public open space. The gardens of the old villas, with fountains, walled gardens and terraces are well maintained and surround the crest of the hill. Sweeping downslope are the broad open swathes of grass but the native oak woodland is its finest asset, Henry's greenwood. There are chestnuts and hornbeams and other native deciduous trees with an abundant underwood of holly. The exotic trees are restricted to the immediate area of the formal gardens.

Springs break out on the slopes and create a muddy halo all round the lower ground, less frequented and less trodden than the upper zone. There is enough space there for a good day's booted stroll and the chance of encountering more than three dozen different species of wild flower. Some of them, like forget-me-nots and honesty, are garden escapes enjoying their new-found freedom of the forest. Busy though it may be, the climb to the hill-top is worthwhile just for the view. From Eaglesfield, for example, there is still farmland to be seen, as well as golf course, cemetery and woodland. Even the river and the riverside suburbs of East London look exciting from this eagle's eyrie. A mixture of images come to mind, a green woodpecker silhouetted against the bare branches of a birch tree, a fox loping along the terrace. Once I met an old acquaintance from Northumberland taking her large black Labrador for a walk. We spoke nostalgically of that northern countryside and its great untouched spaces and she surprised me by saying that she preferred Shooters Hill. No rights of way, no high farming, no pheasant breeding, no lambing to worry about. She and the dog could roam freely, walk where they wished. She reminded me of the ancient link of city and freedom. A year and a day. London and freedom. It never seems more true than in the city's open spaces that are its greatest asset, especially when they are so large and varied as Shooters Hill.

The outlawry of the area had been of concern to medieval kings and, long after Henry's encounter with the bowmen of the greenwood, the forested hills and heaths had such a bad reputation that travellers like Samuel Pepys and John Evelyn preferred the Thames highway as far as Gravesend. But Henry was on safer ground, for down there where the woods sweep down to the south from Shooters Hill lay royal Eltham and another of his palaces. Amongst all the semi-detached comforts of modern Eltham, the village green, the church and the moated site of the royal palace can still be visited. The palace dates back at least to the reign of Henry III though the present Great Hall was built in about 1482. A medieval bridge crosses the moat and rich houses stand along lanes with names as evocative as Green Court, Tilt Yard and King John's walk. New excavations in the grounds of what is now an army establishment are revealing old foundations including those of a chapel. The hall itself is open to the public. Chaucer was clerk of the works at this place and the great Erasmus once dined here. The pilgrim's route along Watling Street is only a mile to the north. The walls of the Hall are lined with prints showing the countryside that surrounded Eltham. Cattle still graze within sight of the Hall.

Of the three deer parks that gave Henry such pleasure and the palace its royal setting, little remains. Once they outrivalled Greenwich in their extent and abundance of deer. During the Commonwealth, the fences were broken, the deer slaughtered, the trees felled. The Great Park, largest of the three, became the private estate of Sir John Shaw in 1663 but now houses the Royal Blackheath Golf Club. A small corner of the park called Tarnwood is open to the public, with a small tarn, a bird sanctuary and an ice-house, one of those curious domed structures that were the deep-freezes of the eighteenth century. The other parks, Middle Park, Horn Park, are recalled only in street names though the abundant playing fields in the area owe their origin to the royal chase.

Another moated house of great interest lies just to the north of Eltham, at Well Hall which belonged to the Roper family. The letters WR are cut into the brickwork, William Roper, Sir Thomas More's son-in-law. One of the last residents was Edith Nesbit the novelist, when the house, one of the outbuildings of the original mansion within the moat, became the venue of many of the literary giants of the time, H.G. Wells, Chesterton, Belloc and Forster amongst them. It became public property and was restored by 1936, for use as a museum and art gallery in what has become known locally as the Dutch Barn.

'Ugly', said Cobbett of the land between Deptford and Dart-ford, the very royal route we have taken. He disliked the new arrivals from the city 'sticking up some shabby genteel houses and surrounded with dead hedges and things called gardens in all manner of ridiculous forms'.[4] He had a fervent antipathy to heaths and wastes and there was a deal of those wild parcels of country. The heaths, wild and intractable, stretched along the ridge of high ground parallel with the Thames, a long lobe of common land that gives South London its greatest amenity and its finest views. The ridge approached the river at Belvedere, aptly named, with perhaps the best view of all looking downstream towards the broadening estuary, lined with industry where the marshes once vibrated with warblers and snipe. Blackheath, Woolwich, Plumstead, Bostall Heath, Lessness form a broken belt of open space even today and all because of their geology, the pebble beds.

The dips and hollows worn by walkers were initiated as gravel workings for building and for ballast, often for the colliers running back along the North Sea to the northern coalfields. There are many piles of flint pebbles from these hills now scattered on the Northum-brian shore to perplex local geologists. Pick up one flinty pebble, smooth and black. It has a long story to tell. It was plucked from the parent chalk rock, the flint smashed by the sea, the fragments rolled and rolled by ancient waters until it joined the other millions in a deposit covering the plateau of South London at about two hundred feet above present sea level. The pebbles show the work of an estuary older than the London clay but younger than the chalk from which the flints were derived. One can only imagine the immense changes of levels in sea and land that have left these river deposits

71

high and dry. Geologists call them the Blackheath and the Woolwich and Reading Beds, up to eighty feet of sand, loam and pebbles. Sometimes they are bound together by lime, making a natural concrete. Fragments of mussel and other shell fragments occur between the pebbles.

Plumstead's 'bare flat of dry gravelly soil, high and breezy' was nearly lost when the manorial lords, in this case Queen's College, Oxford, denied common rights and started to build against local protests.[5] Fences were broken down and, after another long legal battle fought by the Commons Preservation Society, the law found for the commoners in 1871. What is left of the common is marked by a succession of deep coombes that add a touch of drama to the terrain. Nineteenth-century housing creeps up the deep valleys from the riverside and more recent housing advances from the south but the ridge remains high and breezy and the stub of an old windmill forms part of the local tavern. Bostall woods and heath, further along the ridge, were also 'saved' in 1891, a wild enough place to deserve special mention from W.H. Hudson who recorded its bird life. He described Bostall as a spot 'as fresh and unsullied as you would find in the remote Quantocks'.[6] While he recorded the wren, the tree-creeper, the goldcrest and the nuthatch, the only disturbance was from the guns of Woolwich Arsenal.

An earlier traveller in the area, Daniel Defoe, was particularly interested in the woodland 'especially coppice wood which is cut for faggots and bavins and sent up by water to London'.[7] The small, light bavins were used in London taverns to light their faggots. Coppicing, from the French 'couper', to cut, is a common form of woodland management in Kent, by which certain deciduous trees, but especially the sweet chestnut, were cut down to their stubs periodically, encouraging a forest of young shoots to grow from the base, giving a ready supply of small timber for fencing, hop poles, firewood and charcoal. The practice may have its origins far back in medieval times for coppiced woods are the main feature of the woods below Bostall Heath that were owned by the monks of Lessness Abbey, the Abbey Woods. The ruins of the abbey stand on a terrace of open ground by an old shoreline of the Thames, the centre piece of one of the most interesting sites in London, certainly the best of its monastic ruins. North lay the marshes, drained by the monks and pastured by their sheep flocks. The new town of

Thamesmead sprawls over that rich grazing area but the woods are preserved and managed now by the GLC. An ancient mulberry stands by the ruins and formal flower gardens embellish the ruins. The woods in the immediate vicinity have been undersown with spring flowers a blaze of bluebells and, less happily, with cypress trees, a foreign element in an otherwise native scene. Amongst the coppices rise the standard oaks and gnarled hawthorns, birches and holly, rowan, crab apple and wild cherry and other indicators of early woodland.

Though the monastic solitude has gone for ever with the new estates and the bridge bringing hundreds of people to use the recreational area, there is pleasure enough to fill a May day. The tea shop has an information section that gives a guide to the geology and fossils of the area which include sharks' teeth, oyster shells and turret shells, all dug from the pebble beds, the most fossiliferous area in London. The woodlands are made more interesting by a succession of deep, narrow valleys and 'secret' ponds in which a substantial flora survives, bluebells, stitchwort, Jack-by-the-hedge, ramsom, cuckoo pint, ground ivy. A detailed study of the woodland earlier in this century recorded coppicing of ash and birch as well as the chestnut trees. Hornbeam, privet, dogwood, elder, hazel, sallow, buckthorn, whitethorn and blackthorn were all recorded and they can all be found. The wood has changed little from its appearance on a detailed map drawn in the seventeenth century. The abbey was founded in 1178 by the de Lucy family as a penance for the murder of Thomas à Becket. A summer festival held at the end of the month has become a regular feature, with a service, music and dancing. The land came into public ownership as recently as 1930.

Further down Watling Street, the great heaths of Bexley have been covered by suburban housing making the sign of 'The Crook Log' a nostalgic reminder of shepherding days as ironic as the Jolly Farmers in Lewisham's busy high street. Yet a local botanist has recorded no less than four hundred different species of flowering plant in the borough. As the road drops down to the crossing of the river Cray, it approaches another Tudor survival, the flint and stone chequerwork of Hall Place. The dual carriageway cutting through its extensive parkland bears the signpost of the Black Prince. But the royal connections of the house are less certain than those of Eltham. The house is now a library and art gallery, the park a recreation ground but the gardens are almost as interesting as the house itself. Topiary work complete with a line of heraldic beasts leads to a series of small gardens restored in the Tudor style. Sunken garden, water garden, herb garden, rock garden, knots and parterres with low clipped box hedges and yew. The herb garden alone is rich enough in sight and smell to detain the visitor for hours. A foot bridge leads across the river to the comparatively open country of the Cray Valley, effectively London's present boundary. The river, the pastures, the gardens, the nursery and the fine trees attract a number of birds, whitethroats, fly-catchers, chiff-chaffs, warblers and wagtails. The Cray was once the limit of medieval Londoners' hunting rights, according to William Fitzstephen and now it forms part of the Green Belt barrier against the further spread of the city.

The Cray Valley was once called the garden of the garden of England by no less an enthusiast for fruitfulness than William Cobbett, but the orchard country that Henry VIII did so much to foster with the aid of his fruiterer, Richard Harrys, the 'father' of Kent's orchards, has retreated to the farther side of Dartford Heath. The erstwhile fruitfulness of such places as Plumstead is found only in its back gardens though there are few streets without a species of prunus to brighten the scene.

Londoners are often thought to be unaware of the season's change, oblivious of the sky and its subtle variations. Yet every part of the pebble ridge that gives South London its commons and woodlands also gives its inhabitants a panoramic view over the house tops. We each have our favourite. For mine, I return to Greenwich and stand on Point Hill where the mustering peasants could gaze across the meadows of the Thames flood plain to the distant spires of the City. There, in May-time, is one of the finest sunsets in the region.

To the south, the dim outline of the North Downs darkens. On the river below, a coaster drifts silently upstream, the smoke curling to the west. The flags of the *Cutty Sark* flutter bravely like a ship in full sail. In the tree above me, a thrush sings a late song. Starlings speed towards the setting sun, following the gleaming track of the Greenwich railway, the iron line that transformed Deptford's market gardens into one more Victorian suburb. The high trail of aircraft vapour points like a silver arrow towards Heathrow. Then the sun drops slowly towards the City, shadows turn blue, then purple and finally rose-tinted as the sun sinks into a cloud and all colour is washed out until the sun, bigger than ever, falls to the horizon, like a drop of molten metal falling from a cauldron and splashes immediately behind St Paul's, framing the dome in a great fire ball.

Path to Holwood Farm

6

DOWNLANDS

Standing on the edge of Keston Common by the footpath that leads down the steep slope towards the Vale of Keston is the broken stump of a massive oak protected by a railing. From the hollow centre of the old tree grows a vigorous young sapling. There are many other great oaks on that path, still putting out their leaves but that dead tree has achieved fame for, under its shade, William Wilberforce sat with William Pitt in 1788 and gave him notice that he would raise the question of the abolition of the slave trade in the House of Commons. A stone seat opposite bears a commemorative inscription.

The oak stood by the boundary of the Holwood estate which Pitt had purchased as his rural retreat away from the pressure of politics and London. Wilberforce had helped him indulge his passion for landscape gardening. Together, armed with bill-hooks, they cleared new rides through the undergrowth and, in doing so, had seriously damaged the Iron Age earthworks that were known locally as Caesar's Camp. Pitt also had the advice of Humphrey Repton, leading exponent of the landscaping art, to 'improve' his grounds. In order to enlarge them he had annexed part of the adjacent common, a not infrequent occurrence of the time.

Keston's common land, adjoined that of Hayes, West Wickham and Brasted. This extensive tract of woodland and heathland was one of the first to have a regulation act in 1865 saving it from further encroachment. It remains one of the most popular playgrounds for the people of South London. Caesar's Well is the source of the river Ravensbourne and feeds a sequence of ponds that are a child's delight and a mecca for young anglers. With intense use that has reduced much of the area to bare ground like concrete it is amazing that any fish survive and even more surprising that the pond flora includes broad-leaved pondweed and trifid bur marigold amongst all the debris.

The links with Caesar may be apocryphal but there is a substantial Roman building standing in private grounds on the slopes to the west and the Holwood camp was occupied by Iron Age Britons when the legions arrived. The whole area of common land is marked by ancient enclosures and earthworks hidden beneath the present vegetation.

The finest feature of Pitt's estate was the view from the mansion to the south, the 'commanding prospect' which his visitors admired towards the North Downs. That prospect is now entirely within the new boundaries of London. The fact that it is still essentially open countryside is a tribute to the idea of the Green Belt which was first mooted in 1902 by Ebenezer Howard whose commemorative plaque we saw in the Barbican. It was not until 1938 that legislation finally put the London Green Belt on the map, a zone that was intended not only to prevent further encroachments of suburban housing but also, in Howard's words, to preserve 'the fresh delights of the countryside' near at hand. In this area at least the Green Belt has survived for thirty years reasonably intact. The countryside really begins here at Keston.

When I was a boy, that path from the ponds and that oak tree marked the beginning of a new adventure. Behind us was the familiar landscape of pebble beds, the heaths and commons of London's lost villages, much loved but familiar. Ahead was the more exciting landscape of the chalk country. As the closing canopy of woodland shaded out the spring flora and rank growth turned the paths into waist-high jungles so June compensated with an array of flowers, fit for a herbarium, opening on the well-cropped grassland of the Downs.

The chalk holds London in the palm of its hand. It forms the broad basin in which the city sprawls. Its outcrop in the North Downs is matched by its re-appearance in the Chilterns to the north west, rising close to the surface at Ruislip. Even in the centre, close to the Thames at Lewisham, a street called Loampit Vale, where the lime pits were, marks an upward fold of the subterranean chalk.

Many of the shallow pits on the Essex shore around Rainham are old chalk workings.

The southern arc of chalk hills that runs from Orpington westwards to Coulsdon and the foothills of Epsom gives London its best scenery, its finest wild flora and some of its greatest subterranean surprises. As a building stone chalk has never been popular, being too easily eroded by time and atmospheric pollution, though it is found as a rubble infill in the Roman wall round the City and in the windows of the Bishop of Winchester's palace revealed in the warehouses by Southwark Cathedral. But the thick deposits of chalk also contain the flints that supply one of the most attractive and durable of building materials, that grace not only the cottages of the Green Belt but many London churches. Flint was in regular use right up until the first decades of this century. Difficult to use because of their angularity, flints are usually used in conjunction with brick or stone in the corner work.

Parts of subterranean London are as hollow as a drum. Deep mines and miles of galleries occur such as the caves at Chislehurst, an elaborate system of passages and pillar workings that have accumulated legends of Romans and Druids and dreadful deeds that add much to the excitement of visitors. Similar workings occur under Blackheath and were used in the seventeenth century for water supply to the Royal Hospital at Greenwich. Throughout the area, at Chislehurst, Lessness and Joyden's Wood in Bexley, for example, there is evidence of earlier, more primitive access to this underground world, the much-debated dene holes. Many have been filled in and many more underlie housing estates. Heavy rain can cause subsidence and a local scandal. The age and purpose of the dene holes have been the source of as much speculation, as diverse and imaginative as the stories about Chislehurst Caves, including hiding from the Danes. The truth is probably as mundane as chalk working.

Even more important for London is the capacity of the chalk to hold water like a sponge, to act as a reservoir of water just below its streets. There are more than a thousand private wells sunk into the chalk to obtain the deep water. Jam factories, swimming baths, engineering works all use it. One firm told me that the well that reached water at 100 feet early in the century now has to go 400 feet down to find the lowering water table. The Thames Water Authority uses the copious aquifer to augment the supply from the Thames. Northerners often keep a lump of coal for luck. Londoners ought to keep a lump of chalk.

As soon as you descend from the Wilberforce oak, your feet touch chalk, the path turns white and the wayside flora becomes more varied. To avoid the rapidly growing area of Biggin Hill, the best footpath is the one signposted to Downe. It leads through pastures bounded by shaws, the traditional strips of woodland that bound the early Kentish fields as they were 'taken in' from the woodland, to Downe which still bears much the same aspect that it did a century ago 'a pleasant retired village at the intersection of four lanes, the church occupying the centre'.[1] The inhabitants may be Londoners in country guise but the weatherboarded cottages nestling under the shadow of the church, look essentially rural. Near the ancient churchyard yew is a granite tomb that bears the name of one of the most eminent naturalists of all time, Charles Darwin, his name humbly cut beneath that of his brother.

Seeking a quiet retreat and a suitable landscape for reflection after the labours of five years on the *Beagle* and the contention that his observations of nature had aroused, Darwin chose a house and a secluded garden near Downe, eighteen miles from the quarrels of the Royal Society. The local flora and fauna, even to the humble earthworm, became his absorbing interest and his consolation. The house is now a museum to his memory. The hedges along the lanes are exceptionally rich with species, holly, maple, hawthorn, sycamore, dogwood, elder showing their medieval origin, as old as the thirteenth-century church.

The hawthorn, especially after a late spring, is in full flower joined later in the month by dogwood and the sweet smell of elder. The small white clusters of holly flower are waning. The dominant colour of the hedgerow is white matched by the ground flora like stitchwort and parsley with the occasional red splash of herb Robert and campion, woodland flowers that enjoy the greater light of the hedge. Just beyond the house, a footpath leads through pastures and fields devoted to market gardening where the strawberries are ripening readily for London's markets.

Gordon Maxwell, explorer of London's countryside in the 1920s, tells a story he heard from an elderly man in Streatham who knew Darwin. He had heard the great man attributed his good health to his practice of going out into the fields and 'inhaling the sheep'.[2] We can still put this panacea to the test for there are still some sheep flocks to be found grazing their traditional pastures. As the path cuts down through hanger woods, the smell of bluebells still hangs in the shady air. On these busy paths there may be orchids, especially the common twayblade which probably survives because of its inconspicuous green flowering head. But for the most part, the ground flora is composed of yellow archangel, speedwell, common fumitory, cut-leaved cranesbill and the wild strawberry. I say 'busy paths' but I get the impression that fewer people walk these paths than in the pre-war years. Horse-riders are encountered more frequently than hikers.

Between the hanger woods clothing the upper slopes lies the broad smooth-sided valley, the typical dry valley of the chalk. Such valleys, once fashioned by flowing water but now devoid of rivers, have long exercised the landscape scientist. During the ice age these valleys must have suffered a climate akin to that of the tundra of the far north today, the ground frozen, patches of packed snow carrying out their erosive work. With warmer conditions surface water was abundant again and rivers flowed. Now the water table is deep down and only in exceptional circumstances does water rise to the surface in springs. The history of the chalk valleys is a complex one for they may owe their origin to a distant geological time when the chalk strata which had been formed as a marine deposit were folded up into the great dome that once linked the North Downs to the South Downs, some fifty million years ago. As the dome was eroded and the two escarpments were cut back, so the level of the water that the porous chalk contained was lowered and the valleys gradually dried out. The whole of human history is a mere tick in the clock of geological time.

The lifetime of one man seems equally brief when confronted by the two giant yew trees in the churchyard at Cudham where the footpath emerges. One has a girth of more than twenty six feet and the other beats it by just one foot. They are as old as the site of the church alongside, perhaps a thousand years in the growing and they still send out their dark foliage to cover the path from gate to porch. Single yews are encountered frequently; two like these seldom. A local interpretation suggests that they mark a kind of limbo, an intermediate zone between the church and the secular world.

The yew is a common tree of the chalk and abounds in the local woods but in this churchyard you understand their early symbolism of eternity. For the rest, Cudham is a mere hamlet with a pleasant pub, a convenient half-way house on the excursion, overlooking the valley.

Behind the church, a footpath leads north-east for a mile then circles round past hedges bright with spindle to the High Elms estate, once the seat of the Lubbock family and now in the hands of the local authority. The most splendid trees are not the elms, most of which have been felled, but the avenue of tall beeches planted only two paces apart. Some avenues remind you of the nave of a church. This one is a green alley. The house has gone, the parkland made into a golf course but much of the woodland is intact. Nature trails have been laid out and an information centre set up to give greater enjoyment to explorers of this small but varied piece of chalk land-scape. The woods, managed by the Forestry Commission, are mostly of native deciduous trees but plantations of larch and Scots pine lie to the south. A surprising variety of holm oaks are a feature here and laburnum, which came into England in the seventeenth century as a garden and parkland plant, grows wild amongst the beeches. New clearings have been cut to encourage a greater variety of ground flora. Local enthusiasts claim to know the quiet corners where orchids can be found but they wisely keep their secrets.

The elm, unfortunately, is not the only tree suffering from disease. On this estate the Scots pine are affected by chlorosis, a lack of soluble iron, so they are being cleared to be replaced by beeches. Oak wilt, chestnut blight, sooty bark on the sycamores, all leave their melancholy mark. We need to recapture the tree-planting fervour that fashioned these eighteenth-century estates to make up for the ravages of nature and of man.

From High Elms one path strikes north to Farnborough, the edge of the chalk country and the boundary of the built-up area but the circuit back to Keston can be accomplished by footpaths leading to Bogey Lane and the flinty farmhouse at the foot of the Holmwood estate.

On the old Surrey side of the Downs, suburban development has been even more extensive yet it is here at Coulsdon that the best piece of chalk downland survives. Though less than a square mile in extent, its airy setting above the built-up valleys and the new towers of Croydon in the distance make it seem much greater in extent. The first surprise on approaching Farthing Down is the emblem of the Corporation of the City of London, a good fifteen miles from the City itself. The story is a familiar one, of a manorial lord who wanted to enclose the wastes of the manor, who took gravel, marl and loam from the land, sold turf and generally ruined the surface. Then came the counter-attack by others with common rights, a protest movement supported by local subscriptions and finally by the Corporation of London which bought out the manorial rights in 1877 and saved the open space that we now enjoy. An Act of Parliament in the following year gave the Corporation the power to acquire other land within twenty-five miles of the City 'for the recreation and enjoyment of the public'. These included other small parcels of land on West Wickham Common (adjacent to Hayes) and at Spring Park. But Coulsdon's 400 acres was the most important acquisition on the south side of London. Hence the coat of arms, a simple quartered shield with a red cross, appears on the local signs. The same emblem appears on the many 'iron men' in the area and in a radius all round London, more than two-hundred in all of which more than seventy-six survive. These iron posts marked a boundary round London passing which any cargo of coal or wine had to pay a toll for the rebuilding of London after the Great Fire. In 1667 this amounted to one shilling a ton. In later years the revenue was used for rebuilding markets, bridges, drains and other amenities and was finally abolished in 1889. The first posts were set up on the canal entries to the city and then extended to roads and, finally, railways. It is a curious coincidence that those posts almost accord with the present boundaries of Greater London.

Stimulated by European Conservation Year in 1970, the local authorities combined their efforts to improve this area of downland and common with a café, a car park, toilets and other facilities that we now associate with the new-style country parks. An excellent series of booklets has been produced on the bird life of the area, the orchids and the seasonal changes, one booklet for each season. With the decline of common grazing and other traditional usage, the problem today is one of management, of conserving the landscape, the flora and fauna, not only from the increasing number of visitors but from the increase of scrubland and coarser vegetation that compete all too successfully with the more delicate plants. In its own words, the local authority has to do the work of the sheep and the rabbits. The old ways are not entirely forgotten. A sign on Coulsdon Common lists no less than thirty-five offences, forbidding everything from military exercises to 'making improper use'. A list of charges is also displayed, sixpence for marking each head of cattle, two shillings for driving cattle to the pound. The most common species of fauna to be seen today is the horse, for this is within easy reach of Epsom, classic horse country, girding its green loins for Derby Day.

Centre piece of the area is the Happy Valley, a typical dry valley that points its stubby finger south across the London boundary to Chaldon Church with its matchless fresco of Heaven and Hell, and the crest of the North Downs. In the deeper soils of the valley bottom grasses grow tall ready for a hay cut. In the shorter grasses up the eastern slope, the finest chalk flora can be found, the trefoils, the minty smell of marjoram and the small vermilion globes of salad burnet, most typical of chalk plants that was once widely grown in gardens. Put in salads, Gerard, the famous Elizabethan herbalist, declared that, 'it is thought to make the heart glad and merry as also being put in wine to which it yieldeth a certain grace in the drinking.' It makes my heart glad just to see it for the small flower deserves microscopic attention. By St John's Day in the middle of the month, St John's wort adds its yellow head to that of rock rose hiding amongst the buttercups. Searching amongst the increasing hawthorn scrub you may find twayblades, pyramid orchids and early purple orchids. The official booklet lists no less than fourteen species of orchid that may be found in the area throughout the summer. Some, like the early purple, can be found under the coppiced woodland while others, like the bee orchid, prefer the almost bare chalk where there is less competition. So delicate are the orchids in their requirements for successful germination that picking or digging is not only a wanton waste of rare beauty but completely pointless. Other eye-catchers include the common sainfoin, often grown as a fodder crop, looking like a small lupin and easily mistaken for the garden plant which colonises many a waste space in June.

Just as interesting is the flora of Devilsden Wood that covers the western slope of Happy Valley. Oak is the dominant tree but elm, ash and wild cherry are nearly as prolific. The wild cherry, or the gean (a name possibly derived from Guyenne in south-west France) is of special interest. I know of few places where it makes such a fine display. The paths through the wood are well beaten but the ground flora of bluebells, campion, yellow archangel and stitchwort is almost unbroken at the beginning of the month. A small white flower, easily missed amongst the stitchwort, is the woodruff, one of those delectable plants with a variety of country names such as Kiss-me-Quick and Ladies-in-the-Hay. It develops the smell of hay as it dries. Like salad burnet, it is yet another plant that was believed to counter melancholy and a variety of ailments.

Amongst the ground flora and the tangled undergrowth of Devilsden there are unexpected clearings on the upper slopes. There rises the smooth silvery trunk of the beech tree, classic tree of the chalk that outshades all competitors with its dense canopy, leafing long before the oak and the ash. Queen of the forest, some woodlanders call it, not only for its beauty but for the quality of its timber. It does not especially like limey soils but it does like a well-drained one. Its broad-spreading roots make bumpy ridges radiating from the trunk. Most of the beech woods are the result of planting by man, especially in the eighteenth century, but the beech was present in the extensive medieval forests for its mast together with the acorn were the main source of fodder for the grazing herds of pigs, before the forest clearance changed the landscape.

On Farthing Down itself, Saxon burials have been found and the shallow lynchets, low banks breaking the smooth surface of the grassy slopes, are the marks of a Romano-British field system in use two thousand years ago. There are eroded remnants of tumuli which date from even older inhabitants of the windy heights. In all this is a nice outdoor laboratory for deciphering the history of man and landscape not least in the bounding hedges that run parallel lines along the down. They contain all the familiar and many of the unfamiliar hedgerow species, at least twenty, including spindle and whitebeam, with an infinite variety of leaf tint and flower as the month progresses. Using the rule of thumb that the number of species in a thirty-yard stretch gives the age of the hedgerow in centuries, these hedges are the oldest in the London area, dating back to pre-Norman times.

One of the constituents of these chalk hedgerows is the purging buckthorn, with toothed elliptical leaves and a small greenish four-petalled flower. It is essential to the life-cycle of the yellow brimstone butterfly, one of the many species that may be seen in the early days of summer. The chalk blue, the common blue, the red admiral and the large white, the peacock, the orange tip and the speckled wood butterfly may all be seen, flying in the light summer air. Happy Valley is happy indeed especially in the early morning or the late evening when the human visitors are less conspicuous and rabbits and weasels emerge from their bank-side holes, and foxes leave their adopted homes, to glide along the woodland edge towards the ample pickings in suburban Surrey gardens. Foxes usually take over the holes that other creatures have made, the rabbit and the badger. Sometimes they lie up in cover of bramble and may be seen wandering through the woodland, turning over fallen branches or inspecting ant hills. The ant hills may also be plundered by badgers seeking eggs or used by squirrels to hide their hoard. There is also a large badger set in Devilsden Wood.

It is possible to walk, mostly on footpaths, in an easterly direction from Coulsdon's wooded common to two other commons that bear the motif of the City Corporation, first to Kenley Common then down into the Caterham Valley to rise through dense yew woods to Riddlesdown. In these more restricted areas the fauna is often more interesting than the flora. A few quiet hours in one of the secretive clearings between the dark yews and the railway cutting will be rewarded with most of the common and many of the less common birds, a redpoll among the robins, so to speak. The most conspicuous bird, by far, on all these commons is the magpie, floating across the clearings with its striking pie-bald markings and raucous call.

The best of the bird-watching in the chalk area is also on the Surrey side just within the London boundary, the National Trust sanctuary at Selsdon, a mere two hundred acres of woodland and pasture but so managed as to give a variety of habitats, deciduous woodland, pine wood, dense shrubbery and open ground, with nesting boxes and artifical ponds to encourage the birds. In June the young starlings choose the shadowed side of the dense hedgerows for their preliminary patrols, quickly seeking shelter or chasing the adults with open beaks and vociferous demands for food and young fledgling thrushes sit innocently by the pathways.

Simple facilities such as car-parking and toilets are supplied but they are enough to encourage many visitors especially from the local area and this may account for the disappointing ground flora. Some of the woodland is fenced off, the undergrowth kept low and the flowers given space and light to develop but the pastures are rather dull stretches of grass more suited to picnics and ball-games than a nature reserve.

What man diminishes by the sheer weight of numbers, he makes up for in other ways. Nowhere is the contrast more palpable than in the Shirley Hills two miles to the north of the Selsdon sanctuary. There we are back on to the familiar pebble beds, the well-drained, infertile soils that created so much common land, with increasing woodland cover and beaten paths like cascades of pebbles down the steep slopes. Such unpromising materials can be transformed into the most delectable examples of the landscaping art, albeit on a minor scale. On the edge of the plateau are two areas used by the Croydon Council Parks Department for its nurseries and for its training centres. One is on the high ground at Heathfield and one is in the valley bottom in Coombe Wood, and both are open to the public. In Heathfield, as befits the name, Scots pine and heather make the major statements, the heathers abundant in their variety and thrown into theatrical perspective by banks of azaleas and rhododendrons in full and exotic flower. We take them so much for granted now for they are amongst the main floral constituents of every summer park yet they were unknown before the seventeenth century and only established themselves in their present variety and abundance when the exploration of nineteenth-century botanists brought more and more species from the mountains of Asia and other remote corners of the globe. They seem to thrive on well-drained, sandy soils though long periods of drought may be calamitous. Amongst this welter of colour are clipped hollies and, the gnarled trunks of some massive oaks that mark an older land-scape.

The mansion of Heathfield, its stables and out-buildings are symbols of a grandeur that would not have been content with just a pleasure ground but demanded the pride of an extensive park to give it its due setting. The signs are still there in the pastures beyond the privet hedge, studded with fine trees but the panoramic 'prospect' that would have delighted an eighteenth-century squire has been transformed. The pastures quickly give way to pick-your-own strawberry fields and then the suburban rash, with a massive estate plonked down on the summit of the view at Addington. The small flint lodge cottage cowers in face of this architectural anonymity. If the prospect outwards is marred, the inward view redoubles its attraction and you notice the copper beech on the lawn that stands in spendid isolation and the fact that the cut lawn is speckled with daisies while the pastures only yards away are entirely colonised by buttercups, a strict division of floral territory.

Coombe Wood, a short walk down the road or, better still, over the common, uses the same essential ingredients on its higher ground but its heart is in the valley where the garden is divided into a series of 'rooms', rock garden, rose garden, winter garden and broad walk, each with its own character, giving the elements of contrast and surprise. By the end of the month, the rose garden, typical of so many in London, is its supreme feature. This is a well-watered place that used to supply other parts of the estate by conduits and the lane by the main entrance is still called Conduit Lane. It is a cul-de-sac that leads to a bridle path lined with horn-beams and yews and generally gives the impression that rural Croydon is just round the corner. But the path ends in more housing. Coombe Wood keeps its stables and fine farm cart on display and the café can claim the distinction of classical Chinese music and an account settled by an abacus. Available at the café are some most useful pamphlets suggesting trails through the 'living history' of the area which amount inevitably to a nostalgic perambulation through its country past which existed in living memory. The finest reminder of the country days is the windmill with its Kentish waggon-type cap that stands in immaculate condition by the north slope of Shirley Hills, in the grounds of a school. John Ruskin, after whom the school is named, would have enjoyed seeing it in full working order in his country excursions from Herne Hill.

On the summit of Shirley Hills is an observation platform erected to celebrate the Croydon millennium in 1960. Croydon, a thousand years old and more, stands to the west like a miniature City of London, gleaming towers of office, factory and shopping precinct rejecting its rural origins. Arrows on the coping stone of the platform name the most interesting points of that particular compass. There is Harrow-on-the-Hill to the north-west and Epping Forest just east of north twenty-one miles away, the great span of London simmering in the warm days, miles of brick and concrete and tarmac as well as common and park and garden. Yet even on the street, the floral month does not admit defeat. Along one narrow footpath hemmed in by a railway station and a brewery, I counted exactly fifty different wild flowers and grasses. Young heads of bracken were breaking through a recently-laid surface of asphalt. Seven fat pigeons were circling ritually round a crop of shepherd's purse, more purses than flowers, in the cracks of pavements. Ivy-leafed toadflax held its tender flower not on some medieval moated wall but on the concrete side of a drain hole. Ragwort which, like the gorse, never seems to be out of bloom in some corner of the city, has annexed the wastelands and the dandelion clocks are blowing. Altogether more than three hundred species of plants grow in an urban space like Blackheath, for example, including a handful of rarities.

I walk across the heath my shoes dusted with pollen. On the steep bank out of reach of the mechanical cutter, the grasses are reaching their climax, shedding seed; wall barley and false oat grass, timothy standing straight as a poker, Yorkshire fog, soft and delicate. Grass is a major business in the city; different grasses for different uses. The cricket pitches, for example, need a mixture of fescues, browntop, crested dog's tail and smooth-stalked meadow grass. Wherever there is going to be a lot of wear and tear so the rye grasses become the favourites. One inner London borough has listed more than two dozen grasses that can be identified in the area. The grasses are generally not allowed to flower being grown for their close green carpet rather than their fine flowering heads. But they are always around on the edges of the pitches and parks waiting for the sparrows and goldfinches swaying on the stems. If there is one part of the semi-natural scene where the townsman could sound as knowledgeable as the countryman, it is the world of grasses. As they are essentially the origin of our daily bread and our daily milk and, in some cases, our daily beer, they deserve more than to be trodden underfoot without a thought. On the whole I dislike restrictive signs but one I do admire stands at the beginning of a chalk path near High Elms and reads 'Grass is a crop. Keep to the path.' Grass is London's main crop. Prospects of an urban hay-crop are not bright, however. Air pollution, dog droppings and the like make it unsuitable but it may be used successfully as a mulch on bare patches of ground, churned up by the local footballers, for example. In the park, the fescue grass, favourite with the downland sheep, is trimmed and rolled ready for the cricketers, watered into a lush square amongst the browning grasses of the outfield. On the boundary, the holm oaks are shedding their stiff spiky leaves, much to the disgust of the groundsman. At last the streets of the city are really paved with gold under every sycamore and maple and along the avenue the horse chestnuts stand in red pools of fallen blossom.

7

EPPING FOREST

The Guernsey bullock trotted along the pavement until he reached the bus stop. Then he raised his head, eyes glaring, and roared lustily. The small herd of Welsh blacks, Friesians and Charolais looked up in mild interest and carried on grazing the lush grass at the centre of the dual carriageway. So the Guernsey trotted over the road to join them. A number 20 bus glided to a dutiful halt but the Ford Cortina on the outside lane was more spectacular in its braking. So were the fast drivers following it. Happily joined together, the beef herd then crossed the second carriageway on to the grass verge and entered a gateway marked 'Private'. A short grazing expedition into the front gardens was cut short by irate residents waving arms and shouting in urban imitations of cowmen. The herd withdrew and gently, very gently, ambled back across the main road, stopping at tantalising intervals so that any forward movement of the impatient traffic was countered by one more bullock crossing to safety on the common pastures of Leyton Flats that were now turning as brown as hay.

The cattle grazed round the dried-up pond, rubbing their backs with relish amongst the dead branches of last year's burning. A Friesian took a liking to young oak seedlings growing vigorously from the bare ground and its long tongue soon destroyed them. There was little chance for regeneration there. Such pastoral encounters are a daily occurrence on the open spaces of London's northern fringe where the writ of the Forest of Epping still runs. July is the month of the annual round-up when the cattle are marked with the brand of their parish by the reeves who check on the rights

Epping Forrest
Caldecott 82

and responsibilities of the local farmers with common rights in the Forest. Local opinion is divided. To some, the persistence of medieval practices is an anachronism and a nuisance. To others it is a delightful reminder of London's country past. The Forest area, stretching in a continuous sequence of woods and grassy plains from the Forest Gate for more than ten miles to the north, six of them within the Greater London boundary, is the largest tract of countryside available for the pleasure of Londoners. As Defoe wrote more than two centuries ago, 'it may show us, in some parts of it, what the general face of this island was before the Romans landed in Britain'.[1]

A seventeenth-century perambulation of the Forest encompassed no less than 60,000 acres, the last surviving section of the great Royal Forest of Essex that once stretched from the river Lea to Romford and beyond. We are now left with a mere 6,000 acres, about ten square miles. Royal forests were not all woodland. They were 'certain territories of woody grounds and fruitful pastures, privileged for wild beasts and fowls of forest, chase and warren, to rest and abide there in safe protection of the king for his delight and pleasure.'[2] The restored monarch, King Charles II, tried to extend his forest limits, not for the pleasure of his hunting but with an eye to gaining revenue from breaking up the forest and parcelling it out. He failed but the pressure was revived in the nineteenth century and illegal encroachments on the common land became widespread especially after the disafforestation of the adjacent Hainault Forest in 1851 was confirmed by parliament. Local commoners in danger of losing their rights were aroused. They were joined by the supporters of the open spaces preservation movements. The decisive intervention was made, as with the Coulsdon commons, by the Corporation of the City of London.

The City had bought Aldersbrook Farm on the edge of the Forest for a cemetery, a possession that gave them common rights. So when an attempt was made to enclose the waste of Wanstead, battle was joined. The power and influence of the City, in conjunction with the other protest groups, led to the Epping Forest Act of 1878 which preserved what was left of the common and, even better, caused several illegal enclosures to revert to the forest. A visit of Queen Victoria to High Beech in the heart of the forest, set the royal seal of approval, symbolised by the planting of an oak tree.

Stimulated by such royal patronage and encouraged by the Bank Holiday Act of 1871, Londoners took their leisure in the forest glades with tea gardens and pavilions developing into rural 'retreats' for the carriage trade. The railway to Loughton in 1856, and to Chingford in 1873 brought even greater numbers from Liverpool Street and the East End. The motor car has completed the process but the pavilions have long gone. The pubs and occasional tea stalls make a poor substitute for those dreams of Arden. Still, the Forest, patrolled by the uniformed riders of the City, is the haven of high summer, exchanging the heat and dust of the city for the cool shade of the ancient woodland.

Wanstead Flats is not the most beautiful of open-spaces. It is rather a dull, tussocky plain with a few ponds and trees to break the monotony but the cattle can be found chewing the early morning cud by the shade of towering blocks of flats and, as the space that initiated the struggle for the forest, it makes a suitable starting point for a modern perambulation. On the north side of its four hundred acres is a fine avenue of lime trees and a copse of ancient oaks and sweet chestnuts called Bush Wood. The avenue was part of the formal landscape created by Sir Joshua Childs to focus on his mansion of Wanstead Park, much admired by John Evelyn. This had been a short-lived spa area but the water levels kept falling. They still do and the maintenance of the lakes, the central feature of the park, is one of the biggest problems for the City Corporation who gained possession of the park by an exchange of land in 1882. The mansion is gone, its site being somewhere on the nearby golf course but two pillars remain by Overton Drive to give that street an aristocratic entry.

A later owner refashioned the park in more romantic ways, full of dells and lakes, temples and follies. The temple remains but the folly by the lake is ruinous. The lake waters are clean enough to bear water crowsfoot, amphibious bistort and other water flora. The lower lakes running parallel to the canalised river Roding are full of coots and moorhen and mallard, the convoy of chicks making channels of clear water through the green surface of pond weed and algae. The islands used to support a heronry, possibly introduced by the Herons, medieval owners of the manor, but the herons have not nested since the 1950s. Popular with anglers, the park is essentially a recreational space although the intention is to manage it and

maintain it as a parkland landscape of historic interest. Tree planting
has proved relatively unsuccessful, much better results arising from
natural regeneration in fenced-off enclosures, with oak, beech and
hornbeam finding a safe root-hold.

Wanstead Flats are situated on an old river terrace, known to
geologists as the Taplow terraces formed by the Thames and its
tributaries when they were mightier rivers with the great ice sheets
melting from the north, broad deposits of sand and gravel being laid
over the London clay and refashioned by running water. Most of the
local pits and ponds are the result of gravel extraction. Many, as on
Leyton Flats, have been enlarged for anglers. Ponds are honeypots.
They attract large numbers of visitors and the surrounding flora,
subject to incessant treading, dies off. This is true of all the forest
area and the once-prolific flora of the wet zones survives only in the
more isolated reaches of the Forest to the north in Essex.

The Wanstead area is isolated from the rest of the Forest by a
formidable junction of trunk roads but from the Leyton Flats a green
way has been marked with white posts that threads through the
surviving sections as far as the Chingford Plain and the heart of the
Forest in Essex. Each section has its own intriguing name, Gilberts
Slade, Walthamstow Forest, the Lower Sale, Highams Park, the
Upper Sale, the Lops, Chingford Hatch. Within two miles of Leyton
Flats, as the path enters Walthamstow Forest, the two most characteristic trees dominate the scene, the oak and the hornbeam. The
quercus robur, the pedunculate oak, embryo acorns on long stalks,
enjoys the heavy sticky clay soils while the sessile oak, acorns tight
to the twigs, thrives on the drier slopes. There are hybrid species,
too, and another oak, the Turkey oak, introduced in the eighteenth
century, with long, sharp-pointed leaves, colonises like a native.
Acorns were an important source of fodder, essentially for pigs on
the common grazing but they do cattle no good at all, one of the
reasons why grazing is suspended between November and April.

The hornbeam catches the eye, twisted into grotesque shapes.
The tree was seldom allowed to grow to full stature, being either cut
at base, coppiced, or cut at a man's height from the ground, pollarded. These early forms of forest management, cutting on a regular basis, gave a greater supply of timber from the same trees. The
hornbeam, one of the toughest of woods which still supplies butchers' chopping blocks, supplies a slow, hot-burning wood, produc-

ing high quality charcoal. The bakers of Stratford and other North London suburbs depended on the hornbeam from Epping and Enfield. Many of the older trees seem about to fall in half. E.N. Buxton, verderer and author of the standard work on the Forest in the early 1900s, said many rude things about pollarding as a practice and the misshapen trees that resulted. Pollarding weakens the tree by exposing the heartwood to attack from water. Yet those twisted muscular branches rising like arms raised in agony, give the woodland an eerie quality especially in the fading light of dusk.

Highams Park is much more civilised, the woodland tamed into a man-made setting, dominated by a long lake, the glades crackling with magpies. A small child, carefully instructed by a cautious parent, throws bread to six young coots which are using the large leaves of water lily as rafts. The young brood screams thinly for food but refuses to leave the floating sanctuary so the adult birds swim to and fro ferrying the wet bread from child to chick. The father shows the child where another pair of coots are nesting where a bough dips into the water and tells me that more than one clutch has been taken during the season. A pair of great crested grebes paddle safely out of reach of the anglers' rods and delight the child with their elegant crests. Along the path are seats fashioned out of tree trunks, effective, durable and fitting to the scene. Nothing urbane or park-like. Just solid chunks of wood. Even so, some of them end up in the water with the other debris. A mere glade between housing estates, at night it is a highway for foxes, rabbits and squirrels, the common fauna of the urban fringe.

Now the path joins the banks of the river Ching in its meandering journey across the Lops and Hatch Plain. The word 'hatch' often occurs in the area, marking the traditional entries to the common grazing from the surrounding townships. Lops, too, has ancient significance, recalling the lopping rights that were once exercised by commoners, removing wood for fuel. Where the path crosses the golf course is the clearest evidence of the corrugations, the riggs and furrows that, according to Buxton, marked the illegal enclosures for farming. They are not as dramatic as the broad high-backed ridges that indicate medieval ploughlands in much of the English plain. In terms of landscape, they are quite recent. Buxton wanted a method of getting rid of them but they give the golfers an additional hazard and the landscape historian another clue.

Beyond the Hatch, freed from restraints, the Ching winds on a natural course across Whitehall Plain and the flora becomes more varied. For much of the way, we have only encountered those tough, prickly plants that can withstand any amount of rough treatment, the nettles, creeping thistle, dog rose and bramble alive with butterflies, bees, wasps and flies. Along the willow-lined Ching, there is cover for the starry flowers of stitchwort, the marsh forget-me-not, red campion, foxglove, and the common plants of heathland, the heath bedstraw, tormentil and common catsear. Common they may be but each has its special interest. The yarrow, for example, with delicate fern-like leaves and a cluster of white or pink flowers, has links with the great Achilles. The Greek warrior reputedly used it for wounds inflicted by iron weapons, hence its name Achillea millefolium. Juncus rush and a small patch of towering reed-mace, its brown seed heads bursting, fill a boggy hollow.

Turning westwards, the path climbs up clay hills past Warren Pond to the remarkable vision of a complete Tudor timbered building on the skyline, framed with oak timbers from the forest and carved barge boards. Queen Elizabeth's hunting lodge was sited on the summit so as to give a royal view of the hunt on the plain. Now a museum founded by the Essex Field Club, it is devoted to the history and natural history of the Forest. By the main door are two boulders. They may be sarsens, the 'sour stones' or Saracen stones, that are found throughout the south of England, often in conjunction with ancient tumuli, henges and trackways. Several have been found in the Forest and may have been 'mere' stones, marking ancient boundaries. The building itself, a splendid survival, gives great pleasure but here, too, you can check the names of those tall, waving grasses you walked through and the wayside flora.

On display are the tools and weapons of the first hunters, the people of the Middle Stone Age, together with the evidence of Roman occupation and the Iron Age people of the renowned Queen Boudicca. From more recent times are the forest cattle marks of the surrounding townships, showing their rights of stinted grazing, each township being allowed a specific number of beasts. The wild fauna, past and present, appear in photograph and stuffed specimen. The polecat and pine marten became extinct only in the nineteenth century. We could do with the pine marten back as a natural predator on the squirrel which causes such damage in woodlands.

The lodge was also known as the High Standing in its royal days because of its summit site. A long mile to the west across another golf course is an even higher standing, capped by a granite obelisk which marks the true north from Greenwich. Set on a cliff-like edge of the plateau, it commands a view over the London basin to the south as far as the North Downs on a clear day. To the west are the reservoirs of the Lea Valley, broad as an estuary, the old boundary of the counties of Essex and Middlesex.

On a busy summer Sunday, Chingford Plain is loud with model aeroplanes, horse riders and picnic parties but in the early hours it is alive with lark song for the last mile across the level ground to London's boundary hidden in the woodland to the north of the plain.

The oak and the hornbeam are the dominant trees of the Forest with occasional birch and beech and ash, especially on the higher drier slopes around High Beech. Wild service trees and whitebeam, typical of ancient woodland, are also present but they are few and far between. Several can be found in the less-frequented areas like Lords Bushes, an isolated block near Buckhurst Hill. Another feature of the woodland is the abundance of holly, the leaves noticeably cleaner than in inner London. Holly, like bramble, forms a barrier to man and grazing stock and forms a refuge for birds. At its worst, the forest becomes a bare parkland, barren of ground flora, trees encircled by thickets of hawthorn and holly, botanically much less interesting than the forest in which Buxton could record about five hundred different species of flowering plants, excluding grasses, sedges and rushes. The best guide to the present flora and fauna is the information room at the Conservation Centre at High Beech, close by the site where Queen Victoria planted her oak. The centre is run in conjunction with the Field Studies Council and the City Corporation.

Hainault Forest, lying across the river Roding to the east of Epping, was once part of the same wildscape. I remember my first expedition in search of Hainault started with the tortures of the east-bound traffic on the A12 trunk road. When I felt I could stand it no longer, I turned off on a quiet lane to the north and within a few hundred yards found myself in a quiet hamlet, with church and farm and fields of corn, tall and promising, behind hawthorn hedges. I just stopped and stared, thankful for the pleasure comparative silence, the yellowhammers mercifully louder than the distant traffic. The place was Aldborough Hatch which I assumed to be one of the southern gateways to the ancient Hainault Forest. The farmland all round me was enclosed in 1851, following the division of the forest. I noted the names of the farms, Hainault, Park Farm and Fairlop. There was once a massive oak, the Fairlop oak, so large that an annual fair was held under its shade. It was finally burnt down by revellers at the fair. The farmland now is being lost in its turn to the increasing encroachment of housing and industrial estates from Romford to the east and Redbridge to the west.

One of the reasons given in the petitions for the disafforestation of Hainault was the damage done by deer. There are still some feral deer, mostly fallow, roaming in the quieter northern reaches of Epping and some are seen occasionally in the Hainault area but the best herd of deer to be seen now are the magnificent red deer kept in an enclosure in Bedfords Park which covers the hillside overlooking the northern outskirts of Romford. The two hundred acre park, with many exotic trees amongst the native species, was enclosed from the forest as early as the fifteenth century by a Lord Mayor of London. The estate was acquired by the local authority in 1933 and now has a restaurant and a nature trail that leads through the wooded slopes and the pastures on the lower ground, lined with hawthorn and blackthorn. Close by the park is the village of Havering-atte-Bower, another erstwhile royal hunting centre. The village grouped round the green is not as pretty as its name, lacking good architecture but the stocks and whipping post stand in readiness on the corner of the green. The view from the green takes in the entire breadth of the London basin, the North Downs visible on a clear day.

The largest area surviving of the forest is now managed as a Country Park by the Greater London Council and, in summer, the fields bear a heavy crop of visitors' cars, spreading over the pastures. Amongst its attractions are enclosures of ponies, llama, Jacob's sheep, pheasants and the usual exotica that are such a feature of London parks. Most of all it offers space to run in, play in, to enjoy sheer freedom of movement over most of its 1,500 acres, On either side are industrial estates and housing estates that show why such a country park is necessary while the pressures of London's growth continue to invade and transform its countryside. The essence of Hainault lies on the slopes to the north where oak and hornbeam reassert their territory. From the northern edge of the woodland the views take in the rich farmland of Essex where the barley is ripening and the hay cut is over.

Hainault has its counterpart on the west of Epping, on the Middlesex side of the Lea Valley. The Lea, with its broad marshy flood plain, was always a major barrier, a natural boundary between the two counties. It is still a barrier as the view from Obelisk Hill on Chingford Plain shows, the long finger of the reservoirs dividing the wooded ridge of Epping from that of Enfield. The latter had its glory, too, as Enfield Chase in the Forest of Middlesex. The natural link between the two forests lies just outside the London boundary at Waltham Abbey.

Waltham manages to keep its image of a separate place, a small country town but Enfield is firmly locked in the grip of London. On its northern outskirts beyond Chase Side, is one of its loveliest buildings, once a splendid rural retreat on the edge of the Chase. Forty Hall was built about 1700, an architectural gem and now a local museum. The gardens and parkland surrounding it contain some specimens of hornbeam that are larger by far than anything found in the open forest. Suffering no such indignity as coppicing or pollarding, achieve their full grandeur with the characteristic rippling of the trunk that forbids confusion with the beech.

A visit to Forty Hall is not only a delight in itself but a useful preparation for an expedition into the Chase for here is a large collection of prints and maps that show the rural past in detail. John Evelyn had described Enfield Chase as a 'solitary desert stored with 3,000 deer' but it was stripped of game and timber, as were so many royal parks and forests, during the Commonwealth. The partition of the Chase and its sale as 'farms' started then and the area was finally disafforested in 1777. Driving along the hill ridge from Forty Hall to the west, the landscape is very trim and ordered, small regular fields enclosed with hedges and hedgerow timbers, a landscape that is, in essence, three hundred years old. Before that, it looked more like Epping. In the hawthorn hedgerows, oak and elder have colonised.

With the division of the Chase, two estates were set apart and formed into parks. One of them, Trent Park, was granted by George III to his favourite physician. A tall obelisk on the ridge at the north end of the park is inscribed with the date 1702, to commemorate the birth of George, Earl of Harold, son of the Duke and Duchess of

Kent. The mansion is now an institute of higher education and some of the grounds occupied by a golf course but most of the northern half of the park has been designated, like Hainault, as a Countryside Park. Whereas Hainault was created out of farmland and forest, Trent inherited a mature parkland that had been designed for private pleasure two centuries before. The central feature is the lake, sufficiently protected to have yellow loosestrife growing at its side and great-crested grebes nesting successfully. The woodland and scrub reaching down to the south shore is particularly rich with bird life, wagtails, tree-creepers, whitethroats, nuthatches amongst the many tits and finches. The car-parks and other facilities have been put discreetly amongst the woodland on the ridge where, amongst the oak and hornbeam, exotics like the tulip tree appear as if naturalised. Nature trails have been laid out to link the various features of the park but one of the most interesting innovations here is the extension of the trails to include one of the farms to the west on Ferny Hill.

Both Trent Park and the farmland to its north are man-made landscape, two aspects of the countryside that show the modification, almost the subjugation, of the natural world for a specific purpose, for amenity in the first place and for the production of food in the other. A wilder aspect by far survives on what was the western extremity of the Chase in the common of Monken Hadley. The parish boundary is shaped like an arrow, enclosing a share of the chase of about 240 acres, granted to the township when the land was divided up. In its course from the village church down to the valley, the common changes its aspect from trim cricket pitch to open heath, succeeded by dense woodland. It has the distinction of having three toll-gates on its perimeter though they seem to be purely decorative now. The village is as interesting as its common, nicely grouped round the church. The 'monken' part of its name comes from the possession of the township by the Abbey of Walden. Yet another extensive green lies to the north of the village that was the site of the battle of Barnet between the Earl of Warwick and Edward IV, an episode in the War of the Roses.

The southernmost extent of the Chase is found in London's suburbs at Southgate, literally the southern gateway to the Chase. There are several parks, Oakwood Park and Winchmore Hill, that owe their origin to enclosure from the ancient common.

London is full of names that show its forested past, when the oaks gathered their strength from the stiff London clay. I have spent many an hour poring over maps, noting a name and then exploring. Acton caught my eye. Acton, acorn, the oak town, the town among the oak trees. Old Oak Common is still marked to the north of the place, to the western side of Wormwood Scrubs. Only a hundred years ago, James Thorne reported that 'the village is clean, quiet and rather picturesque, observe the fine flowers in the cottage gardens'.[3] Acton still has a green and a village church and there is still a street name, Wells House Road, to recall its fashionable wells on the side of the common. But the last great oak was cut in about 1831. The common was once used as a military training ground and I am not surprised that the soldiers were often up to their knees in mud. Oak trees enjoy good, thick, sticky clay. Soldiers don't.

If Londoners cannot get out into the forests, chases and farmlands of its bounding countryside, then some enlightened local authorities bring the countryside into the town. Lambeth Borough Council holds its Country Show, now an annual event of spectacular proportions, in Brockwell Park one of the most complete eighteenth-century parklands in South London. As befits a borough that bears such a country name, the lamb hythe, it offers the sight of a red-faced shearer plying his skill with hand-cutters on a herd of Romney sheep, the heavy six-pound fleece falling from the protesting animal while the onlookers ask how much it costs, what does the beast weigh, does it hurt, how many can he shear in a day and the shearer takes it all in his stride like a good performer, his hands slippery with grease from the raw wool. In the arena, four sheep dogs try their paces, herding the terrified sheep round for all to admire, ushering them through hurdles and into pens, the onlookers voicing their envy of the shepherd's skill and the dogs' patience, while the hundreds of spectatorial dogs fret and groan. When it's all over, the heroes of the half-hour snooze in the back of a van, quite detached from the mêlée of pipe bands, motor bike teams and panting steam traction engines. The beer tents do a roaring trade while the tents crammed with fresh milk and farm produce entice us all to healthier diets. The horses jump round and round and round and craftsmen show their quieter skills. A farrier fashions a horse shoe and fits it with the coal gleaming red and the smoke rising with an acrid smell amongst the great oaks that stud the park. To the north the gleaming towers of London look so close yet so far away in spirit.

In the side stalls, the rural reminders accumulate, showing us how to make corn dollies, thatch a roof or keep bees. Self-sufficiency is all the rage. Windmills turn again in anticipation of the day when the fossil fuels run out and we all revert to the simple life. In other tents, local societies display their collections and old maps show that Brockwell Park itself was once farmland and that the Effra, one of London's lost rivers that flowed past the park, was once called the Shore. The flight of three tree-lined, duck-filled ponds that run through the park fed into that long-lost river. The badgers roamed here, too, hence the 'brock'. Brockwell came into public ownership on Whit Monday, 1892, the mansion still intact and the walled garden now being transformed into an Old English garden, the forerunner of many more to come.

ear Holwood Farm
Keston
O Caldecott 82

8

LONDON'S FARMS

The biggest horse I have ever seen was cantering around in a circle at the end of a halter rope on a fine August morning on Clapham Common. His jet black coat shone in the sunlight. His white 'feathers' hanging from the fetlocks had been washed and powdered. Eighteen and a half hands of power, he looked strong enough to carry a medieval knight in full armour but now that strength was harnessed to pulling a brewery dray. It was the morning of the Greater London Council horse show and the dray horses were amongst the major attractions. The big shire horse I had been admiring had his stables down where the river Wandle meets the Thames at Wandsworth, on a small farm complete with geese, ducks, guinea fowl, peacocks, goats and the brewery mascot, a short horn ram. A further twenty magnificent shire horses complete the unusual collection by London's riverside.

An even more palpable link with the crown of the farming year is in a large tent at the Horse Show, in a quiet corner far from the thunder of the hunters, hacks and riding horses leaping over a variety of obstacles. Landrace sows sprawl in complete relaxation with litters of piglets suckling, sheep and cattle breeds snuffle amongst the hay and the fruits of the earth are displayed in all their richness. There is a smell of carts and dung and tractors and the big, burly men have the tanned faces of those who spent their life out of doors. Most of them are tenant farmers of the Greater London Council from farms on the north-west fringes of London in the ancient county of Middlesex.

Clapham is one of a group of commons including Tooting and

Wandsworth that were sliced up by railways development in the nineteenth century and land lost to housing, hospitals, asylums, prisons. Clapham fared better than most because of rival manorial claims for grazing and other common rights. Even Battersea staked a claim. Clapham had the reputation of being one of the best regulated commons, well drained, planted with trees and generally kept in good order. Nineteenth-century prints invariably show cattle grazing on its two hundred acres. So the Greater London Council brings back the sights and smells of the countryside to where they once belonged.

The days are long gone when Hackney was famous for its turnips, when Battersea cabbages and Deptford onions filled the stalls of the Borough Market and Covent Garden. It is more than a century since the main fruit belt included Kennington, Hammersmith and Isleworth but the last milk cows did not leave the City itself until 1953. Though the fields had gone, the cows stayed on, stall fed. In the 1930s there were still more than one thousand in inner London, eighty-five of them in Bermondsey, giving the freshest of milk to the roundsmen who measured it out daily into the customers' churns. When the new London County Council was formed in 1888, there were still 745 cow-houses and ten thousand cattle in its administrative area including one in St John's Street, Clerkenwell. At that time, my grandfather kept a goat called Betty and a pig called Patsy in the back yard, together with the chickens and rabbits. The nearest grazing cow is less than a mile away, through the Greenwich foot tunnel to the Isle of Dogs.

The grazing on twenty-eight acres of deserted dockland would not bring delight to a modern dairy farmer but the waist-high lushness of every conceivable wasteland weed is grist to the goats' mill. This year's crop of young kids prance around the remnants of wartime ammunition dumps creating an impression reminiscent of one of the wilder corners of the Balkans, an impression heightened by a flock of Jacob's sheep advancing over the skyline. Only when the eye-level is changed and the cranes and warehouses of Millwall Docks come into view does the bravery of the venture become apparent. Even the donkey has safely delivered its young much to the delight of local children. Never were country images more acceptable. Local children descend from the tower blocks complete with riding habit for a canter round the retaining banks. My own delight in the area was crowned by the sight of a pair of wheatears circling me, birds that I associate with the moors of Northumberland. Wheatears are not unusual during the migration season but this pair had decided to adopt this strange patch of dockland moorland as their summer home.

Mudchute is not unique. There is another small farm using the waste ground of Surrey Docks, modifying a dockside building in what must be one of the most unusual farmhouses in Britain. The donkeys, hens, ducks, geese and bees are not just for show but give a supply of eggs, yoghourt, cheese and honey, and the goats are available for clearing anyone's garden. There is a similar venture in the Royal Albert Dock. While the more grandiose schemes for the redevelopment of dockland are discussed endlessly, small groups of adventurers bring the countryside back into the city. Perhaps when small is beautiful once more, the rural scene will find rebirth in the garden city and the season's rhythms be reflected by more than the price of produce in the local market. Sheep grazed in Hyde Park until the 1950s and wartime necessity turned many a wasteland into productive use. I have heard, too, of a bee-keeper within sight of the Tower of London who finds the quality of the City honey superior to that of his Essex hives.

Such small but delightful diversions apart, it is quite a task to find the nearest working farm to the centre of the City. The Epping cattle graze seven miles away at the nearest point but the general radius is between twelve and thirteen miles, to Aldborough Hatch in the north-east, Enfield in the north and Bromley Common in the south. The nearest I can find now is to the south-east, nine miles away at Eltham close to the moated palace. Medieval Londoners could reach farmland in a ten minutes' walk. It is not just the distance of the farming fringe that is so dramatic but the speed of its retreat. My first suburban home was close by a river with watercress beds and two mills. My second was part of an estate built on a dairy farm. School rugby could only take place after we had cleared the pigs off. Street names like Farmstead Road are the only tangible reminder. The steading itself was allowed to fall into ruin. 'When the old farmhouses are down, what a miserable thing the country will be,' wrote Cobbett. A little imagination could have preserved some of the old farm buildings as a reminder of the rural past and our final dependence on the produce of the land. The buildings were more solid than many that have taken their place.

How refreshing it is to walk through the recreation ground at Headstone in north-west London and find a massive wooden barn and a manor house in a moat, two remarkable survivors from an active farm that the local authority intends to preserve and adapt to modern usage. They make everything about them seem dull by comparison. Becket may have stayed in the moated site when the land was held by the archbishopric of Canterbury. A working farm with a large dairy business stands only a half mile to the north, at Pinner Park, but the track through it reveals a farm so industrialised that it looks more like a factory than a farm. Beyond Pinner is the largest area of farming land in the Greater London area, In the reorganisation of local government the GLC inherited nearly ten thousand acres of farmland that had been acquired by the old Middlesex County Council. In 1931, a conference of the home counties studied the loss of rural land. Middlesex was especially affected, not only by roads and railways but by the extension of the underground system to Stanmore, and so the council bought up much of the remaining farmland. This was the first effective step in the creation of the Green Belt which received statutory authority in the Green Belt Act of 1938.

Agriculture is still the main use of the green belt land in the borough of Hillingdon but the loss of farming land to gravel extraction, building and new roads would lead, at its present rate, to a complete extinction of farming by the year AD 2000. As we travel in search of the last of the rural countryside, we recall wistfully John Norden's declaration in 1593 that 'the soil of Middlesex is excellent, fat and fertile and full of profit'.[1] While there are patches of top-grade farmland between West Drayton and Heathrow Airport, most of the surviving farms have to make a living on medium grade land, nearly three-quarters of it devoted to grass with the emphasis on dairy cattle. Considerable efforts are being made to improve that farmland despite pressures on it. As the planning reports point out, 'A neglected farm does nothing but harm to the basic conception and high ideal of a Green Belt.'[2] Prosperity makes a better landscape than poverty.

Farming on the urban frontier has more problems than the fluctuation of milk prices and the aberrations of the weather. It faces damage from thoughtless vandalism and the ignorance of the country code. Horse trampling, dog worrying, broken fences, gates and stiles are part of the daily round. In an effort to improve the situation, the Greater London Council has encouraged its tenant farmers to open farm trails which can be followed by visitors. Two are in the vicinity of Harefield, at Park Lodge and at Knightscote Farm. The former has been made into a Farm Centre with a massive milking parlour at its heart, designed to give a grandstand view to parties of visitors. The farm is one of three run as a single commercial unit, with 250 cattle and 150 sheep on 500 acres.

The farm trail guide to Knightscote Farm, which is a model of its kind, informative and well produced, points out that 'grassland management is an art'. The land is only of medium quality, developed on heavy clay soils with a high water table, requiring drainage and skilled and persistent effort to grow crops. Rye grass, fescue, timothy and cocksfoot become names to conjure with for they can be translated into better milk yields. Once the grasses are chosen, and sown, then the most suitable breed of cattle must be brought in.

The most popular breed in the area is the British Friesian, a dual-purpose beast that gives a good milk yield and calves that can also be raised to produce beef. The paddocks are grazed in rotation, then rested and fertilised. Then in the wetter months of winter, the animals are stall fed to prevent excess tread or 'poaching' of the pastures. Occasional fields of oats and maize add to the total fodder available. Modernisation and mechanisation has enabled two men to do the work that once needed eight. This is no cosy rural scene but the mere sight and smell of cattle and grass gives it an amenity value that is emphasised by the local planning authority. Patches of old woodland and hedgerows that have lost their original function are retained whenever possible. Most of the hedges have between six and seven species in a thirty-yard length, suggesting enclosures of the thirteenth and fourteenth centuries, an area of late farming clearance of the forest. Many of the farm names have a medieval ring for this was part of the Breakspear estate, the only English family to supply a pope to Rome. The estate was purchased by the local authority in the 1930s. On this farm, I found two wild service trees, one in a hedgerow, showing the antiquity of the woodland cover. By the farmhouse are two staddle barns, small storage barns raised on stones, which are at least two hundred years old, taking us back to the days of horse and hand labour.

Harefield is a useful starting point for exploring the Middlesex farmland. As a village its best feature is the square four-acre green, typical of the thirty or more greens that existed in the county. In most cases they can still be found trapped like fossils of previous ages, for greens like commons were the subject of medieval rights, their ownership much more complex than that of the surrounding farmland. So Acton and Ealing and Wood Green can still sport their village greens. Harefield's green serves one of its traditional functions when the August fair arrives. But the buildings round the green, apart from the inn which manages to retain some rural charm, do not deserve close attention. The high street, too, is unexceptional until it slopes down towards the isolated church of St Mary and there on the left stands a brick building of great beauty, a Tudor house built round a courtyard, with a fine cluster of chimneys.

Just beyond the churchyard is the beginning of a footpath, generally well-signposted, that leads due east not only through typical farmland but to the best woodlands and open spaces in the district. The elm was the main hedgerow timber and the edges of the fields sometimes resemble a graveyard of trees so the sight of Bayhurst Wood one mile to the east is all the more reassuring. Bayhurst is the best parcel of woodland in the north-west, a survivor of the old Forest of Middlesex, similar in composition to Epping, with oak and hornbeam dominant and a variety of other deciduous species such as the elm, the beech, the birch and one or two wild service trees, botanically speaking a very ancient wood.

Bayhurst, which deserves to be regarded as a nature reserve, has been developed as a Country Park complete with barbecue site right in the heart of the wood. Toilets, car park and horse rides show the new 'positive' approach to such areas. I wonder how the woodland will stand up to the treatment. A better area for such development would have been the next woodland that the east-bound path reaches, that of Mad Bess Wood, less interesting botanically but more extensive with large areas of coppiced hornbeam and chestnut and many good walking tracts. Only a secondary road separates Mad Bess Wood from Copse Wood, equally large, with the footpath leading down hill towards the Ruislip Lido in the valley. Between the wood and the lake is a piece of common land called the Poor's

Field, dedicated in 1804 to the use of the poor of the parish.

After the shadows of the August woods and the carefully controlled farm landscapes, this common tract has welcome wildness, a
display of wild flowers with heather, agrimony, harebell and petty
whin, none of which are common in the London area. In the stream
bed, water plantain grows tall, bearing its characteristic white,
three-petalled flowers. On a hot, gorse-popping day, the warblers
are flitting from cover to cover repeating their incessant plaintive
call. The keeper here assures me that he has seen the white admiral,
a rare high-flying butterfly, in the glades amongst the oaks, together
with the purple hairstreak and other insect delights. The common
has not been grazed since the 1950s so there is much shrub colonisation especially by oaks which are bearing the long light lammas
shoots as befits lammastide, the beginning of the month.

The soils in this area vary from London clay, to Reading Beds
and even include glacial gravels nearer the stream. The flora, which
reflected such diversity, has suffered from the encroachment of
scrub as well as from the heavy tread of feet on the way to the
pleasures of the Lido which began as a reservoir for the Grand
Union Canal. An area to the north of the Lido has been enclosed as a
nature reserve. Ruislip itself is a busy town, the effective edge of
London's built-up area but it retains a sufficient number of good
buildings, barns and timbered cottages round the church for this to
be designated as a conservation area, the old village core of the
parish. There are several footpaths leading back from the Lido
across the farmland towards Harefield to provide a walking circuit.

Overgrown tracks lead westward from Harefield down to the
river Colne and the Grand Union Canal with much lusher meadows
and a genuinely rural view as soft as a Corot painting, enhanced
rather than spoilt by the colourful pleasure boats on the canal. The
valley is now the westward boundary of London, twenty-five miles
from London Bridge. Disused gravel workings have been transformed into a succession of lakes, bright with yachts and anglers'
umbrellas, a new Country Park to cope with the increasing quest for
country recreation. This broad valley was, no doubt, the site of the
two mills and four fish ponds with no less than one thousand eels
recorded in the Domesday Survey of Harefield, the complement to
its land for five ploughs worked by ten villagers and three slaves and
its woodlands extensive enough to support more than one thousand

pigs. Woodland, ploughland, meadow and river; the walk has traversed the entire medieval sequence.

There are hints of an even more ancient countryside elsewhere in Middlesex and none better than Harrow in its isolated hill with its old township land stretching to the north to the forested weald bounded by a long linear earthwork called Grim's Dyke. The very name of Harrow the Saxon 'hearg', indicates a heathen temple site that may have been adopted by the later builders of the Christian church. The present church is largely post-Norman, a site where Becket once held court shortly before his martyrdom and a church which dominates the skyline in a way reminiscent of the continent. Despite later encroachment, Harrow has the look of a separate place, a town on a hill surrounded by greenery. That green halo is now marshy playing fields and golf course, but an active dairy farm adds to the rural illusion. The common land round the hill was enclosed after 1803 and nearly all the surviving hedgerows are dominated by hawthorn with an occasional mixture of holly and maple. By the tomb of John Peachey the young Byron sat and wrote

High through these elms with heavy branches crowned,
Fair Ida's bower adorns the landscape round

The elms are gone but fortunately the same spot is embowered with lime trees, their delicate flowers falling.

Harrow had common rights in a much larger area of woodland to the north, in Harrow Weald which survives despite nineteenth-century encroachment. On the way there, by the roadside in Weald-stone is a large recumbent stone, a massive lump of conglomerate like concrete. Like the sarsens of Epping, this may have been a boundary stone and, in view of its position, it is tempting to see it as a marker between the ploughed land and the woodland. Harrow Weald, like the town on the hill, owes its eminence to a capping of gravel beds on top of the London clay, a situation we have met at Hampstead and Highgate, resistant to erosion and, because of their infertile soils, resistant to the plough. The Weald's forty-four acres, added to the hundred and twenty acres of the adjacent Stanmore Common, create a wildscape on London's northern boundary, an area of great amenity value where more than twenty different species of butterflies, and more than thirty breeding birds have been recorded. The flora is not spectacular in August due to the dense shade but the native deciduous trees are enriched by the exotica of the Grim's Dyke estate which was developed by Sir William Gilbert, of operatic fame. One of the notable introductions amongst the prevailing conifers is the strawberry tree, an arbutus that bears fruit like the strawberry. The greatest visual appeal is of the native rowan, very prolific here, its berries red with the promise of autumn. The keeper of these woods is an enthusiast, a real lover of trees, in whose company the whole place achieves new significance. He showed me where the rabbits had attacked the beech trees, debarking them and the efforts he had made to repair the damage by treating the wounds. From the fallen birches he creates the most rugged, attractive seats that line the paths.

The northern limit of the Weald is marked by a ditch and double earth bank, a fragment of the long alignment of Grim's Dyke. Its origin, like that of the wealdstone, is uncertain but if it bears any relationship to other long-distance ditches such as Offa's Dyke, it may have been a boundary dug in the early Anglo-Saxon period when Harrow got its name and the county of the Middle Saxons took shape. The banks are lined with the gnarled shapes of pollarded hornbeams.

Stanmore Common has areas of clearing amongst the woodland, the additional sunlight encouraging a greater variety of flora especially the heathland communities of tormentil, stitchworts and a patch of common ling. Tormentil with its four small yellow petals may have derived its name from its ability to 'torment' such unpleasant ills as the colic, its roots being boiled in milk as an antidote. Walking the bounds of Stanmore, within sound and sight of the M1 motorway, you can find linnets and yellowhammers approaching as close as town sparrows and spotted flycatchers patrolling the woodland edge in their incessant search for insects in the sultry air.

The early spelling of Stanmore indicates 'mere' rather than 'more'. There are few wet zones on the common but one pond by the cricket ground is clean enough to bear amphibious bistort. The mallards grab hold of the pink flowers, dunk them under the water, shake them, gobble and then release them to bob up again above the surface.

'All Middlesex is ugly', declared William Cobbett, but the beaux of the town would not have agreed with him. Not that he cared a fig for their opinion, preferring the company of the itinerant labourers he met, scythes over their shoulders, moving from field to field, cutting the grass crop. But in the southern part of the county nearer the Thames were four of the most fashionable summer retreats, villas set like jewels in parkland with all that money, art and good taste could provide, a world away from the drudgery of the farms. In the desire to cap their neighbour, nothing new in the London suburbs, an element of competition grew up, expressed in many a contemporary verse such as one by Sir William Pulteney,

> Some cry up Gunnersbury,
>   for Sion some declare,
> Some say that with Chiswick House
>   no villa can compare;
> But ask the beaux of Middlesex
>   who know the country well
> If Strawberry-hill, if Strawberry-hill
>   don't bear away the bill?[3]

Strawberry Hill must keep its laurels to itself for the house is now part of an institution of higher education and much of the ground built over but the other three are available to the public to spend the summer days and compare their relative merits. No villa can quite compare with Chiswick for it has been restored by the Department of the Environment as the quintessential Palladian villa. Yet the nuance is not of Italy and the Grand Tour but of Egypt. Children clamber over the stone sphinx in glorious disregard for its position as part of the exedra, the open-air avenue of statuary and trees that was inspired by Hadrian's villa at Tivoli, where the Roman emperor surrounded himself with memories of travel to Egypt and the far-flung empire.

The house, too, with stone floors, ornate ceilings and classic doors bears the same feel of an eastern mausoleum, a strange, cold place in contrast to the warmth and life of the grounds. Burlington, patron of the arts, was the owner and every fashionable name concerned with landscape art was involved, Inigo Jones, Samuel Wyatt, Colin Campbell but especially William Kent who wrote a new chapter in the history of landscape art. The formality he planned, with crow's foot of radiating avenues lined with yew, has grown romantic and rugged with time but the formality is supreme in the Italian garden, a picture in every sense of the word.

Chiswick is comparatively withdrawn, still a dignified retreat that was often used as a royal residence. Gunnersbury was royal once, the summer retreat of Princess Amelia, daughter of George II, whose parties were celebrated. The present mansion was built in the nineteenth century by Baron Rothschild who maintained the tradition of splendid parties, according to contemporary writers. The mansion is now a museum and a meeting place and the park is so busy in summer that there is little chance to indulge in the contemplation that Chiswick inspires. With all the furore of summer pleasure the little temple by the round pond looks quite incongruous.

Though Osterley is not celebrated in the same party-goers poem, it deserves even more present praise as an Elizabethan hunting park containing a Robert Adam mansion and enough space in its lakes and woods to make a sanctuary for wildlife, even so close to the M4 motorway. More than eighty species of birds have been seen, including the first breeding record of the great crested grebe which has now spread into other London parks. The trees planted near the house include cork oaks as well as the more usual cedars and planes. Some of the great trees, especially the beeches, one dominating the lawn, are now past their maturity and falling into their death throes. The restoration of the parklands is as important as the restoration of the houses for they are both essential features of created landscape.

Syon has the finest pedigree of them all, site of a medieval monastery and heir to one of the earliest botanical gardens. William Turner, known as the father of English botany, wrote the *Names of Herbes* at Syon in 1548. Sections of Tudor walls and mulberries in the private section of the park survive from Turner's time. On one of the main lawns stands a statue of Flora, Roman goddess of flowers, as befits an estate that has been famous for its gardens for five centuries, and has acquired new fame as a garden centre in recent years. Some of the trimness of the last decade has been modified and a new informality achieved more in keeping with the tradition of Lancelot Brown, the Northumbrian landscape gardener who transformed the grounds on behalf of a Northumbrian duke in the second half of the eighteenth century. Many of the trees which Brown used to 'punctuate' the landscape are still there but his masterpiece, as with many of his gardens, was the lake, nearly a quarter of a mile of serpentine water which not only creates the visual centre piece but carefully controls the water supply through the estate from Isleworth back in a long loop to the Thames, functional as well as beautiful. Every path opens new vistas, in keeping with the original intention, peacocks trailing their tails through the shrubbery, swamp cypress and catalpa boughs sweeping down to the water's edge, holm oaks bringing a reminder of the Mediterranean, yucca from further shores. This is a work of art on the grand scale. Although the full beauty of its conjunction with the Thames can not be enjoyed from the public area, the view from the house towards Kew redresses the loss.

Syon, Chiswick, Osterley and Gunnersbury contrive the perfection of the fashioned landscape. They give us glimpses of countryside beyond our ken. They were all dependent on the older, more workaday countryside of farm, field and forest. Middlesex can still offer us both.

9

WATERWAYS

There is a general agitation in the air. The gulls are massing on the heath. Three hundred starlings follow the fresh swathes of the mower and dig their beaks into the soft soil. Pied wagtails arrive in small flocks instead of their usual ones and twos. Above them all, the martins seem to grow in numbers every day, their thin, high-pitched screams becoming more and more insistent. They swarm above the horse chestnut and then, towards the middle of the month, suddenly, they are gone, leaving behind a few stragglers with their late broods gathering strength in domed nests under the eaves of the Victorian villa for the long journey south. The annual migration is on.

In the park, the regular patrons have returned from their holidays, bronzed with the summer exertions. The jog-trotters, the dog-walkers, the duck-feeders are back on their beats. In a dip in the contours of the park there is a specially quiet spot with trees close enough together to give a copse-like appearance, with abundant hawthorn and holly, and a small watering place at the bottom of the dip. In the early hours, the first risers become aware of birds on the move, not the massed exodus of swallows as seen at Beachy Head or of terns from Dungeness but the quiet movement of single birds flitting from cover to cover. A whitethroat tumbles around a hawthorn, searching, searching, never still. A spotted flycatcher launches into an insect-grabbing foray. Two willow warblers hop from hawthorn to holly. Inexorably the general movement is south and west, the hedge-hopping migration of small birds escaping the winter. Sometimes there is greater drama, a flock of a hundred or

Camden Lock
©Caldecott 82

more meadow pipits descend on the level ground in front of the Queen's House, stay for an hour and then depart.

The autumn migration is easier to observe than the incoming movements of springtime. The flocking is more obvious and builds up during the opening hours of the day. That dark, swiftly-moving cloud over the city just after dawn may be chaffinches or skylarks in their thousands. Fortunately for the observer, such flocks sometimes alight on one of the large open spaces to rest and feed. It can happen at any time from late July onwards, depending on the weather, reaching a climax in the first weeks of September. The main movement seems to follow the Thames valley from east to west but subsidiary routes have been identified along the tributary river valleys from north to south, such as the Lea, the Colne and the Cray. Even the inner London valleys like that of the Wandle offer a variety of open spaces for the migrant birds to take a breather, in parks and playing fields, on commons and reservoirs and, especially on sewage farms. Sewage farms are the mecca of the September bird-watchers.

Specific flight lines have been noted, as sharply defined as aircraft corridors, one, for example, over Primrose Hill, Hampstead Heath and Regent's Park. Many of the common birds of the city, the wood pigeons, the blackbirds, carrion crows and chaffinches, are involved in migratory movements but the greater excitement is raised by the chance of seeing the uncommon species which are seldom seen at other times of the year. Then rare sightings may occur even in the inner London parks, avocets, little auks, hoopees and firecrests amongst the pigeons and sparrows. Woodcock, snipe, whimbrels, and warblers are enough to bring the enthusiasts out of their comfortable beds. On one such occasion I saw a red-headed bunting sitting in a hawthorn bush on an outer London common. Even rubbing the sleep out of my eyes, I could not be mistaken for the bird is striking in its colouration, and it sat still long enough for me to get the identification book out of my pack with fumbling hands. This native of the Caspian shores, admittedly a rare visitor to Western Europe, was much more likely to have been a caged bird on the loose, than a genuine migrant, but it made the day memorable.

The Thames itself is one of the most important points of transit and the sighting of Chelsea Reach, for example, may be more varied than at any other time of the year with pochard, tufted duck, wigeon, teal, pintail, scaup, goldeneye, smew with the even rarer arrivals like goosander, merganser, razorbill, gannet and the occasional puffin, enough to make the watcher drop the identification book in sheer excitement.

One of the bird-watching valleys is the Wandle that runs from Croydon to Wandsworth and the most famous site on it is the Beddington sewage farm. Modernisation of the plant has reduced its attraction to birds but some of the land retains the aspect of a marshland, a rarity in London much prized by the wet-zone birds like the snipe which has been observed in thousands. The grounds are fenced off and opened occasionally to organised groups of ornithologists but there are other open spaces close by such as Mitcham Common and Beddington park which can do service for the layman like myself, content with lesser treasures. I was taking cover from a heavy downpour in the scrubby, neglected ring-belt of trees that borders the east side of that once fashionable park. Water was dripping steadily from the browning leaves of the horse chestnut which was my shelter. A motley flock of birds hustled in from the direction of the sewage farm, sought the sanctuary of the inner branches, ruffling their wings and feathers vigorously. Goldfinches were most prominent amongst them, the most characteristic bird of the month, plundering the seed heads. A whitethroat appeared among a mob of tits. A wren stalked along the hedge beyond the ditch and a hawfinch tried out its beak on a just-ripening hawthorn berry. A song thrush, beautifully speckled, preferred the first of the yew berries. The hedge sparrows avoided cover and swept over to the cricket pitch which still had its stumps up and melancholy pools of water all round them.

It felt like autumn, all very ordinary but all very enjoyable for a wet hour. Then the rain was gone and summer made a brave return. The cricketers came out to test the pitch and four little boys persisted with football by the boundary line. The birds departed as swiftly as they came, back to the no-man's-land behind the factories and the sewage works where horses munched along the raised banks and yellow wagtails patrolled between them. The experts would expect a much greater harvest than that for the records for Beddington include curlew and dunlin, knot, sanderling and ruff, black-headed gull, redshank, lapwing and teal, birds of the estuaries and marshes, the wilder shores of England brought for a moment to a London suburb.

The great mansion in the park is now in public use and by its side stand the buildings of the old home farm, a particularly fine dovecote and a 'cottage orné'. Beddington still has a village hall, post office and a pub happily called the Harvest Home, appropriate for a September visit. My last call coincided with the village tea party which, for its friendliness and sense of neighbourhood could have been in the heart of the Weald. Home-made cakes and hot strong tea put the wet day to rights. The broad open spaces that follow the course of the Wandle cannot disguise the fact that the valley became one of the most industrialised rivers for its size in the world in the late eighteenth century lined with ninety mills producing cloth, gunpowder, paper, copper, calico. So busy was it that the Surrey Iron Railway was built along its length after 1803, a far cry from being a royal fishing preserve in the seventeenth century when Michael Drayton could enthuse about its clear waters 'so amiable, so fair, so pure, so delicate'.[1] The sewage works opened in 1860 completed the industrial pollution yet there were still the visionaries who saw a better future for the valley.

Octavia Hill, whose energies had been directed to the protection of City churchyards, to new parks and the protection of the common land, pioneered the idea of a green walkway linking the existing green spaces along the Wandle. 'If pleasant walking ways could be provided radiating from the crowded suburbs, what a blessing they would be to pedestrians,' she wrote and the River Wandle Open Spaces Committee was set up in 1911.[2] The scheme failed but the concept lived on to find fruition in our own time in other London valleys. On the lower stretches of the Wandle there are just three small pockets of open space owned by the National Trust, Wandle Park near the site of Merton Abbey, Watermeads and Happy Valley, both near Mitcham Bridge: Happy Valley was given as a memorial to Octavia Hill. What pleasure her walkway would have given now, linking the brewery farm at the river's mouth with the park at Beddington.

The walk is still worthwhile. There is the conservation area of Merton, with medieval church, an arch and wall surviving from the priory, and memories of Nelson. On the edge of Mitcham Common, on the Lower Green, is one of the most famous cricket grounds in the country where the game has been played for 250 years and names like Sandham, Strudwick and Richardson are listed on Tom Ruff's memorial. Stumps will be drawn at 6.30p.m. said the notice. At 5.30 on a dull September day, I could scarcely see the ball but the batsman could, judging by his successful attempt to get the ninety runs needed for victory, maintaining the traditions of the giants of the past.

A similar idea for a riverside walk was mooted in the enthusiasm of post-war planning by the Boroughs of Lewisham, and Deptford along the river Ravensbourne which had plentiful meadows and eleven watermills. The sites can still be identified; one, by Southend Pond, supplied cutlery with a national reputation in the eighteenth century and another, the Armoury Mill, at Lewisham, was linked with the Tudor navy at Deptford. The demand for housing, however, meant that the flood plain of the river, so long and so wisely left undeveloped, became built over. But rivers have a habit of flooding their plain and the Ravensbourne, such a puny trickle for much of the time, has swept straight through Lewisham High Street on more than one occasion. Now the river has been tamed, at much expense. The mallard and the pied wagtails have not deserted their haunt by Lewisham Bridge despite the new concrete bed of the river.

In the last decade, Octavia Hill's riverside walkway has been realised in the form of Country Parks developed along two of the Thames tributaries, both within the London boundary, one in the west along the river Colne and one to the east, down the river Lee. The Colne Valley Park is the most rural of the walks, essentially a tow-path walk from Harefield four miles south towards Uxbridge with all the pleasure that lock gates, canal craft and old bridges deeply grooved by the rub of a thousand tow ropes along the Grand Union Canal can provide. The Park, set up in the 1960s, concentrates on water sports, from angling to sailing, most appropriate to an area between canal and river that has a string of lakes on flooded gravel workings. Extraction of the flood plain gravels is still proceeding but the disused pits are the basis of the new leisure pursuits. The varied water surfaces are also an attraction for wildfowl and birds on passage. It's a poor day if you don't see heron flapping lazily into the air or cormorants, necks stretched out, in fast, purposeful flight over the water. Walking south from Black Jack's Mill, one of the best mill sites in London, there is scarcely a quarter of a mile without its patch of reed beds or flooded marsh to provide the perfect warbler territory with reed buntings, wagtails, bullfinches, chaffinches, tits and woodpeckers in abundance. Great-crested grebe dip and dive in the quieter embayments under a massive willow, while the swallows and martins glide and turn with infinitely more dexterity than the boats beneath them. Towards Denham, there is an especially good stretch where the river and canal run close together with a wooded, often flooded, zone between them where the exotic parkland trees are mixed up with the tangled vegetation of the wet zone. The flora along this section reminded me of the purer rivers of Sussex levels with purple loosestrife, arrowhead, flowering rush, common water plantain, trifid bur marigold, watermint, teasel and a host of more common waterside plants. Late summer is much more prolific than the early season, attracting a late flush of butterflies and other insects. Particularly notable is the orange balsam which spreads along the banks, a plant which propagates itself by exploding with ripeness and scattering its seed. The plant originated in North America and is now naturalised along London's canals. The sight of the M40 flyover ahead is a disincentive to proceed further south but, happily, at that point, by the junction of the Colne and the river Misbourne, a footpath leads north west towards Denham, a picturesque village just outside the London boundary.

The Lee Valley Regional Park is an even larger, more adventurous concept. It starts in rural Hertfordshire with cattle grazing on the flat meadows around Waltham Abbey but quickly enters the industrial zone that leads to the heart of London's East End. Starting from Enfield Lock, just within the London boundary, there is a full day's walking, a good twelve miles down to the massed football fields of Hackney Marshes. The unifying thread is the tow-path of the Lee Navigation, linking an almost continuous sequence of open spaces, reservoirs hiding behind high embankments, parks, rough meadows that will one day support new leisure pursuits, unkempt corners of side canals and locks that may become nature reserves. Set up in 1966, the Regional Park is primarily concerned with the realisation, to quote its own brochures, of a fifty-two week holiday area with sailing, cycling tracks, horse riding, golf courses and leisure centres to give effect to Abercrombie's war-time planning dream of 'a great regional reservation'.

123

For much of its route, the canal is lined with factories, metal-working mills blazing with green flames, timber yards, waste paper and the like but the sheer width of the Lee flood plain, more than a mile in places, is enough to break the visual domination of urban structures. There are many places like the heronry at Walthamstow that, with the advice of the Royal Society for the Protection of Birds, will give sanctuary to breeding birds as well as a highway for migrants. There are more than 68 breeding species recorded by these extensive reservoirs including such rarities, so far as London is concerned, as the gadwall and the shoveller, ringed plover, little ringed plover, lapwing, water rail, red-legged partridge and king-fisher. Apart from the partridge which is a bird of farming land, the others are typical of the species which need a specialised habitat, with water meadows and marshland as the attraction. Permits from the Thames Water Authority are needed to penetrate the best areas but the birds are often observed in the more public places.

In the middle of an unoffical motor-bike circuit in the rough grassland by Hackney Wick, I met a man in a Securicor van who had his binoculars trained to the skies. A gentle, kindly fellow, he spent all his holidays in the highlands of Scotland watching birds of prey yet seemed almost as happy to spend his off-duty hours in this urban wilderness. He spoke of hobbies and buzzards passing through and enthused about a corncrake sighted that morning. Not a bird of prey, he hastened to add, but a secretive bird worthy of his attention. He preferred the high fliers and drew my attention to a kestrel hovering above.

This area offers one of the best chances of seeing the black redstart which finds the tangled apparatus of power station, gas works and metal factory as hospitable as the rocky uplands of Southern Europe.

The canal-side flora in the first few miles to Ponder's End is almost as rich as the Colne with masses of arrowhead, bistort and trifid bur marigold showing the comparative purity of the water. Purple loosestrife, watermint and tansy follow the wet channels on the adjacent meadows. Water-forget-me-not and great willowherb fill an old lock. Clutching the canal bank itself are the welcome colours of Himalayan balsam, orange balsam and gipsywort. Thickets of elder massed with berries, hawthorn, alder and willow line much of the route. As we move south so the flora gets less interest-

124

ing, golden rod and the giant hogweed amongst the thistles of Hackney. It is possible to mark the boundary of each of the species showing the changing conditions from truly rural to entirely urban. When the Regional Park has completed its massive undertaking, we may find tansy and trifid bur marigold moving south to Hackney.

It would need a determined walker to follow the Lea to its meeting with the Thames but one day, if present plans materialise, he will be able to follow the Lea Navigation to Hackney, pick up the Hertford Union Canal to Victoria Park and do another twenty-eight miles along the Regent's Canal and the Grand Union ending up in the Colne Valley. This watery walkway link between the two country parks is taking shape. Westminster Council opened up a mile from Lisson Grove to Primrose Hill in 1968, linking up with the section to Camden Lock, which was added in 1972. The new paving stones take away some of the atmosphere of the old tow-path but the wapitis and the gnus on one side and the exotic aviary on the other make it look like a canyon where the deer and antelope roam. In this section it is the sparrow sitting on a hawthorn and the sow thistle by the St Pancras boundary stone that look like the intruders.

When John Nash was the driving force behind the Regent Canal Company, this waterway navigated the perimeter of London. Towards Camden past the bridge where five tons of gunpowder blew up in 1874, informative plaques on the brick walls supply a running commentary on the history of the canal and draw attention to such points of interest as the horseslips, long ramps that enabled horses to get out of the canal once they had fallen in. Among the buildings lining the canals are the lock-keepers' cottages and the inns that once gave sustenance to the navigators. Now they supply a more affluent clientèle and are amongst some of the most attractive corners of the urban landscape. The wayside flora, facing the severe restrictions of brick and concrete in place of earth banks, is so adaptable that I recorded nearly as many species as the Colne Valley could offer in the same length, including toadflax, alkanet, penny royal and hedge mustard. Two of the most notable invaders, adventitious flora brought up in canal cargoes, are the bladder senna with a flower like a yellow peaflower with a very distinctive papery pod, and the Japanese knotweed which has become a coloniser of waste land and even of London commons as far afield as Stanmore, producing a head-high jungle of angular stems.

Another notable section of the canal with a rural flavour lies beyond Perivale contouring round the conical outcrop of Horsenden Hill, yet another eminence that owes its survival to a residual capping of pebble beds protecting the more easily eroded London clay. This straggly open space with a suspicion of an Iron Age earthwork on its summit and a golf course on its flank, is one of the best viewpoints in West London. A reservoir built to supply the canal at this point lies four miles north-east, the Brent reservoir, better known as the Welsh Harp not only to the sailors who exploit its exposed choppy waters but to the thousands of bird-watchers who frequent its banks. Close by the Edgware Road, its bird life must be the most closely watched in London, if not the country. The quiet zones for birds are surprisingly small and the debris of the city as prolific as the reeds and rushes that give the birds shelter and food. Nevertheless, its strategic situation makes it a port of call for dozens of species, grebe, pintail, smew, pochard, Brent geese, barnacle geese, wigeon, coot, tufted duck, warblers, finches, tits. The latter include such rare sightings as the bearded tit, so called because of its dark markings on either side of the beak, more like a moustache than a beard.

The Brent is fed not only from the heights of Hampstead but also from the small Silk Stream flowing from Stanmore. In turn, it feeds south-west through Wembley, Park Royal and Ealing where it becomes the section of another canal leading to Brentford. Golf courses, allotments and parks follow the river and one section at Hanwell has already been raised to the status of the Brent River Park. Hanwell is an unusual spot, its Victorian church and village core being at the end of a cul-de-sac. Seen from the river meadows, snowy white with seed fall from the black poplars, it looks like rural England, an image soon dispelled by the popularity of its park, its caged birds, rabbits, donkeys, sheep, monkeys and owls. The old park is the centre of the new 800-acre river park.

The tow-path walk along the Brent Canal, which includes the famous Hanwell flight of locks, is part of the overall plan, a great boon to a part of London that has borne the full brunt of the city's westerly growth. In John Rocque's 1762 survey, Hanwell is a village eight miles from the city. A hundred years later the urban fringe was still six miles away.

London's rivers are a constant source of interest, especially the minor tributaries like the Silk Stream from Stanmore. Some of the 'lost' rivers like the Fleet, the Tyburn and the Walbrook are well known, but who except the local historian would know the course of the Falcon, the Effra, the Beverley Brook or the fine-sounding Neckinger? Respectively they are to be found in Battersea, Lambeth, Richmond Park and Bermondsey. There is still the faded sign of the Neckinger Mills at Bermondsey to mark the river that lapped the walls of the monastery. Too many of London's rivers have been degraded into unseen channels. Cities need rivers. They are the essence of the natural landscape. Long may the Wandle wander through Beddington Park even where it floods, as I saw it one September day when the sandbags were hastily erected around a new housing estate. The Brent meandering by Hanwell Church is a delectable hazard for the golfers whose tee-shot drives straight across its widest meander. How pleasant would the City be now with the Fleet lapping below Ludgate Hill!

One of the few places where a river follows a comparatively natural course, meadows sloping down to earth banks, willow-lined meanders winding through gravel terraces to the Thames is the Cray Valley between Foots Cray and Bexley on the Kent border. The Cray was regarded as one of the most fruitful, tranquil valleys in the garden of England, and, as such, became lined with a succession of great houses and parks, amongst them one of the finest Palladian villas in England, built by a Cheapside pewterer. Lord Castlereagh lived and died on the adjacent estate at North Cray Place. The landscape of the Cray reflects the fashions of the eighteenth century, ponded stream, ornate bridge, avenues of limes and chestnut and exotic trees on the terraces where the villa once stood.

The source of the Cray in the chalk springs by the church at Orpington is the best part of that Saxon village which has transformed itself with twentieth-century speed into just another towny suburb, complete with shopping parade and the inevitable precinct. For three miles the river lurks behind housing and industrial estate but from Foots Cray it becomes a valued part of the Green Belt, despite the dual carriageway that speeds traffic towards the Dartford tunnel. Watercress, water parsnip, water pepper and hemp agrimony are flecked with the first tumble of willow leaves drifting downstream. Yellow and grey wagtails patrol the muddy banks, turning over wet leaves, run and peck, tail bob, leaf turn, then a quick dart over the water for an insect before resuming the mudlark, with elegant strut and tail firm. Then they zoom high above the willows, moving south. Many wagtails remain for the winter but a proportion, especially of yellow wagtails, are migrant.

On the islands, lined with reedmace, by the bridge, the coots have raised a last brood, their voices sharp as pistol shots. Moorhen and mallard leave the meadow and plunge for safety in the reeds. Two tumble off a floating milk crate while a sudden flash of kingfisher leaves an indelible memory, seen so briefly but never forgotten. Red Admiral butterflies drop delicately on to the fresh dandelions and the evening air is filled with dragonflies.

The attraction of the area is enhanced both for ourselves and for the birds by the presence of one of London's largest planted woodlands, a mile to the east at Joyden's Wood, linked to the river-meadows by footpaths and bridle paths. This is the nearest Forestry Commission plantation to central London with areas of open heath amongst the pine, spruce and larch. Bracken dominates the undergrowth but some heather remains along the much-frequented rides and scabious is in full flower when everything else seems to be fading. Hawfinches and whitethroats flit through the piny darkness and two large mistle thrushes sit on a young Scots pine and look as impressive as kestrels. They are only an inch or so smaller than the bird of prey and their direct flight can be misleading in the dusk. In places the Woolwich and Reading Beds have been leached into a hardpan as tough as iron but the chalk is not far below the surface and the older wood to the south, Chalk Wood, shows a different composition of trees and ground flora.

The Forestry Commission has railed off several areas in an attempt to restrict the erosion caused by the legions of riders in the vicinity. Outside the woodland edge, the corn crops are gathered and the last stubble smouldering. The dewberries are bold and the blackberries full of promise as the jam-makers follow the hedges with their plastic bags. The sun sets over a strange amalgam of London's outer fringes, glasshouses, market gardens, stables, factories, houses and the subdued silhouette of a church spire, a last salute to village life.

10

DEER COUNTRY

Just one hundred yards from the car park, a fine red stag takes his ritual stand by an ancient chestnut tree gathering a harem of twenty-one hinds about him. He nuzzles a hind, licking his lips constantly, moving through the herd. All seems calm in the cold dewy morning until another stag appears under a hawthorn some fifty yards away. The stag, gleaming polished points on his antlers, brow, bay and tray and three on top, a truly kingly crop, turns towards the intruder, lifts his head back, Adam's apple bulging, nostrils flared and groans wildly. The sound is so harsh that it sounds as if it dragged out of his very being, echoing across the park. More young stags move close threatening his omnipotence. He charges after them in short erratic runs, turning swiftly to guard the hinds. He stands and stamps his feet, paws the ground with fury and thrashes the earth with his horns. When he lifts his head, he has tufts of bracken and grass draped all over him, looking quite ridiculous until he starts to run again and the grass flutters from his antlers like a green mane. The competitors retreat and the victor stands, head down in near exhaustion, by the tree. Such sound and fury can last for days on end, the stags unable to eat. Such is Richmond in October, the setting for the most remarkable event in London's natural calendar, the rutting of the deer, a time of wildness that the park boundaries scarcely seem able to contain.

There are herds of deer in many London parks, all, except for Bedfords Park at Havering-atte-Bower, fallow deer usually with a solitary buck and a small harem of does. Even without competitive males the October agitation shakes the ground whether in Clissold

Park or Charlton, Golders Hill or Victoria Park. The buck roars up and down the small park enclosure stamping his feet, eyes flaring, throat swelling, giving the Sunday promenaders a hint of some primeval order of things and they move instinctively to a respectful distance. But it is in the wide open spaces of Richmond Park that the full majesty of the annual drama is portrayed.

Richmond Park is not only the finest open space in the London area, it is flanked by other spaces of such quality, Bushy Park, Ham Common, Putney Heath and Wimbledon Common that in any other area they would be notable. Here they are just one part of a matchless wildscape with the sights and sounds of the ancient countryside, the smell of birch and bracken, the birds massing for winter, badgers seeking a mate and foxes sniffing the night air, ten square miles of some of the loveliest landscape in England. It is possible to plan a walk of nearly twenty miles from east to west all within London's boundary and feel the soft give of grass beneath the feet, with a mere mile of roadwork and always be within the sight of trees. The blunt silhouette of tall buildings, the sound of the highway come as a surprise, such is the enchantment of the route.

A suitable starting point is the green at Wimbledon at the north end of the oldest and most attractive part of the borough, once the village on the hill or 'don'. To the north and west lies the common, possibly the best in London. At first the route is tame past a round pond besieged by model boats and young anglers glaring at the ducks, an avenue of trees alongside comfortable houses but soon the common takes over with scrub oak and birch and a mass of spiders' webs draped over the gorse bushes like silken handkerchiefs left out to dry. Then comes the first patch of heather. Heather, the common ling, is now a comparatively rare plant in London, being almost absent from many of the heaths where it flourished a century ago. It is easily shaded out by other plants, by scrub and trees and that most successful competitor, bracken. Heathland is a result of a specialised type of management, of cutting and burning in keeping with ancient practice. When the old uses of the commons decline, when the grazing stops and the gathering of fuel, so the vegetation changes and reverts eventually to open woodland. Unless the London heaths are managed carefully the only heather we shall find will be the planted clumps in local parks. Fine as they may be, with cross-leaved heath, bell heather and Irish heaths competing for attention, they are no substitute for heather in its native habitat. Heather for luck, lucky for Wimbledon.

The wanderers with a passion for archaeology will take the path due west by the golf house towards Warren Farm to see the fading circular ramparts of the British Iron Age camp that the Lord of the Manor once tried to erase from the landscape. He put up a scheme for the improvement of the common in the 1860s with the proviso that Putney Heath to the north should be sold for housing to pay for the improvement. After strenuous local protests, the whole tract was saved in 1871, with its camp, its burial mounds, its windmill and its historic heritage. The Board of Conservators had, and have, the task of maintaining it in as near its present natural state as the pressures of the public use will permit. That pressure can be seen on every path that crosses the wasteland that once formed an essential part of the economy of the surrounding manors of Wimbledon, Putney, East Sheen, Battersea, Wandsworth and Clapham. The trees dropping their branches in the October winds recall the windfalls that the poorer commoners used to gather for fuel. On Michaelmas Day at the end of September, the beadle used to cry 'The common open', open for the collection of firewood and the like until Lady Day in the following March when he would cry it shut. But the maltsters and bakers used the wood, too, and timber was often cut green in abuse of the common code. The holder of a virgate of land could graze five cattle, fifteen sheep and two pigs on the common, a poor cottager only two cattle, a pig and a small horse. The lord of the manor retained the right to dig for gravel, hence many of the damp pits which not only provide the present ponds but the richest flora with marsh pennywort, trifid bur marigold, skullcap and lesser spearwort though most will be past flowering by October. We shall be lucky on the open ground to find more than Michaelmas daisies, smooth hawksbeard, heath bedstraw and purple moor grass. The view to the north-west is already dominated by the silhouette of the windmill and the past suddenly becomes the present.

The mill at Wimbledon is unique, the only remaining hollowpost flour mill in the country. And if you are not sure what that means there is a very good display inside the mill about the whole history of mills, the post mills, the smock mills and the tower mills that ground the corn until the last century with illustrations and examples of such milling mysteries as wallowers, governors, miller's willows, crooks and rods to put you in the picture. The mill has been restored with loving care since it ceased to be used when the Spencers sold out their rights to the Commoners. There was much competition from the water mills of the Wandle and the Hogsmill at Kingston. The miller here was also the Constable, on the look-out for robbers and duellers on the common. Putney Heath lying to the north of the windmill was the site of probably the last duel in London, between Prince Louis Napoleon and Count Leon. Open at week-ends, the mill alone would make a visit to Wimbledon worthwhile. It is more like a mill hoisted up on top of a cottage. It was sub-divided into several dwelling houses, not vacated until 1974 when the restoration of the mill was undertaken in earnest.

There are other windmills in the London area, for example, the tower mill of Brixton built in 1816 and working until 1934, now restored again and open to the public, close by Brockwell Park. There is another tower mill at Shirley in very good shape, in the grounds of a school, dating from about 1860, and another at Barnet. Parts of a smock mill can be found in St Mary's Lane at Upminster dating from the last years of the eighteenth century, shown also by a model in the Romford Library. But the oldest to be seen is the post mill, where the whole structure revolves round a central post, or used to, on the edge of Keston Common. It is in a sad state of decay, standing in private grounds, but it can be seen from the common. Dating from about 1716 it beats even Wimbledon by a century. There are, of course, many old stubs remaining like the pub on Plumstead Common called the Mill, and another at Barnehurst.

The Wimbledon windmill is left reluctantly not least because of the excellent cup of tea at the adjacent café. The path to the south-west is not easy to follow. There are always the hazards of golf but even more the many coombes confusing the terrain of the wooded slopes. I always find myself on a different track but usually find the small monument to the memory of the men of the Royal Rifle Corps and remember that the common was the venue of the crack shots before moving to Bisley. That must have been an even greater hazard than golf. The tracks lead down through oak and hornbeam, chestnut and hazel, holly and rowan over well-trodden gravel to Beverley Brook, one of the most sylvan streams in London though the beavers that gave their name to the stream have long since

133

departed. We may encounter foxes, rabbits, weasels and even Brock the badger but beavers are just a river's memory. Where the wooded slopes give way to the playing fields on the level ground there is a large monument standing in an exact circle of oaks, and a flock of long-tailed tits bustling past. The inscription reads 'Nature provides the best monument, the perfecting of the work must be left to the gentle hand of time'. Already that forty-two acres has lost its formality and fits easily into the broad pattern of the waste, all of it a monument to the endeavours of the past to keep some of London's erstwhile countryside available to future generations. That is to say, us.

After a brief but sobering encounter with the twentieth century in the form of the main trunk road to Portsmouth, the A3 and the Robin Hood roundabout, the gates of Richmond beckon. Beyond lies 2,500 acres of freedom, only two green miles in the straight traverse but this is no space to be crossed by the shortest route. Richard Church felt that a very profitable summer holiday could be spent just exploring the park. A summer holiday? A lifetime would not exhaust its possibilities for Richmond has magic at every season but October holds a special enchantment when the trees are full of melancholy and the deer are at the peak of their activity. This was once Sheen Close, a royal hunting ground, emparked and walled in by Charles I when the land became Richmond New Park. He annexed some common land to enlarge the park which did not add to his popularity. Some of the great oaks may date from the earlier hunting ground, older than the present walled enclosure. An oak can be two hundred years in the growing, two hundred standing still and take another two hundred to die which simple formula may put some of the leviathans back to the fifteenth century at the least.

The Commonwealth, which disparked many of the royal hunting grounds, kept Richmond intact and gave it to the City of London. It was returned to the Stuarts with the Restoration. Public access has been granted ever since apart from minor interruptions such as the time of Princess Amelia, George II's daughter who became the park ranger. She lived in the White Lodge which was built by her father. It has been used frequently by royalty since and was the birthplace of George VI, father of the present queen. Between the Robin Hood gate and the White Lodge lies Spankers Hill Wood, a nineteenth-century plantation, and a small enclosure of gorse. It may seem strange to protect a patch of young gorse but it is all part of the scheme to give birds more sanctuaries and feeding areas. Many seed-bearing trees and shrubs were planted in the 1960s with the same purpose for Richmond is one of the richest areas for bird life in the city. October may be too late for the warblers, whitethroats and blackcaps but the quiet walker may see magpies, woodpeckers, jackdaws, starlings, hedge sparrows and house sparrows, little owls, kestrels, crows and even redstarts, yellowhammers, skylarks and pipits. At the last published account no less than ninety-eight species of birds were recorded, fifty-six of them as breeding species, more than any other royal park. Only in Richmond will you find the water rail, the jack snipe, the barn owl and the garden warbler. Even the stonechat, bird of the heathland, circling from bush top to branch with its constant warning like two stones knocking together finds enough solitude to stay and raise its young.

Perhaps the most prolific bird area is the Isabella plantation in the south-west of the park, an enclosure of exotic trees and gardens and water, where even the woodcock has been sighted, a garden where autumn colour reaches its climax but, in its variety, quite unlike the rest of the park which is dominated by the greenswards and native trees of the past. All paths seem to lead to Pen Ponds, the largest of the water surfaces held in a grassy basin in the centre of the park. Carp, dace, perch, bream, eels and pike fill its waters and many visitors line its banks, so take one of the less-frequented routes north-west of the White Lodge across the harebell-speckled spaces towards Bog Lodge, one of the favoured centres for deer, the red stags taking up their 'stands' by the same trees year after year. Sometimes in warm October days, the stags are content to laze in the tall grass and raise their magnificent heads to groan as if in ritual obeisance to the rut, almost indifferent to the movement of hinds, but as the temperatures fall and autumn bites, they are roused to their usual fury. Then the older, stronger stags stand and groan their challenges, gathering the females about them while the younger stags gather at a respectful distance. By one chestnut tree, the ground bared by constant pawing, one stag gathered no less than forty hinds about him and, as the competitors approached, groaned constantly. In his ferocious energy, he covered one of the hinds several times. As he did so, another hind moved away towards another stag and the chase and the stamping of wild feet proceeded. At its peak, the noise can accompany the walk all the way from Richmond to Hampton, echoing across the river Thames. A herd of fallow deer moved between the competitors but they seemed quite oblivious of the intruders.

The fallow herd is 350 strong while the red deer number about 250. The red are the royal deer, the only herd in London apart from the handful at Bedfords Park near Havering. The male is the stag, the female the hind and the young are calves. For the fallow deer, the males are called bucks, the females does and the young are fawns. There is no mistaking them. The red are much larger beasts and their antlers bear shining points while the antlers of the fallow are shaped like blades. The coats of the red are at their best, truly red before the winter change. Their antlers are proud and shining, freed from all velvet. They are smooth from constant thrashing of trees, especially the hawthorn, often doing considerable damage to trees, marking their territories and anointing them with their scent. Many trees are protected by railings but others are left to this essential purpose.

There is no mating between the two species. Their rut is just one of phase but the fallow bucks will be just as agitated before October is out. The culling or killing of selected animals is carried out to maintain the quality of the herds and to prevent overgrazing of the park. Man is the only predator now. Some of the venison, by tradition, goes to the Prime Minister, some to the Archbishops and other favoured recipients, but the rest goes to Smithfield for commercial sale.

To the west of Bog Lodge is an area of willows leaning with age, of hawthorns grazed by the deer into strange shapes of natural topiary, of cockspur thorn bearing fat berries, of oaks on the woodland edge. There can be moments here when one has the sense of being in an ancient countryside, older than farming, older than the plough, what England once was. It is all an illusion for the aircraft from Heathrow are humming overhead but such moments enrich the spirit and tease the imagination. The privacy of such areas attracts the smaller fauna of the park, the foxes, now so common that their numbers have to be limited, weasels, stoats, squirrels, hedgehogs, rabbits and hares. There are common shrews, pigmy shrews, bank voles and field voles, active in the quieter hours but the pride of Richmond are the badgers, and there are believed to be eight active sets. Badgers like extensive grounds for their feeding territory but need privacy and safety and, like the fox, are finding suburban habitats more suitable than the open country. There are fewer enemies. In recent years, several have been recorded in suburban gardens often occupying old rabbit warrens. The grounds of hospitals and other institutions are tailor-made to their needs. Wimbledon Common is as close to the city centre as they have ventured yet.

The path curls easily westwards past the Richmond Gate towards Pembroke Lodge, its gardens and refreshment rooms. This is a most popular corner of the park, the entrance to the gardens being marked by a plaque to James Thomson, poet of *The Seasons*, who found echoes here of his home on the Scottish borders. In the gardens, on the edge of the river cliff above Petersham and the Thames floodplain, is Henry VIII's mound, an artificial mound possibly constructed for a view of the chase but now commanding a panorama of the Thames Valley with Windsor Castle to the west. A few hundred yards away the view to the east takes in Westminster Abbey and St Paul's Cathedral amid the commercial towers of London. Richmond is happily poised between the two royal palaces.

West of Pembroke Lodge, the ground falls sharply away like an inland cliff to the flood plain of the river Thames and some of the loveliest villages and villas in London. The geological map poses questions for glacial gravels are mapped on the higher ground of Richmond. We can imagine the ice and its meltwaters pounding up against this cliff-like edge and the first hunters gazing at the broad raging waters of an early, mightier Thames when primitive man was gathering a bleak sustenance in a harsh world. Now it offers the softest, most civilised landscape imaginable with pearls like Petersham giving the best of both worlds, a rural retreat within an hour of the city centre. The temptation is to drop straight down that wooded slope to the riverside but the better route lies due south along the rim of the plateau, savouring the wilder delights of the deer park as far as Ham Gate. To the west lies yet another wooded common, lined with an avenue of trees until two lodge cottages with Dutch gables mark the meeting with the seventeenth century. From the lodge stretches a mile-long avenue of limes and elms that was once the main approach to the palace of the Earl of Lauderdale, a Stuart favourite.

Ragged and unkempt at first, the avenue, still a right-of-way, gathers strength until the destination at Ham House, now in the possession of the National Trust. The gravel terrace that fronts the river is lined with pineapples made from Coade stone, with the centre piece of the river god, very clean and resplendent, fitting the setting to perfection. The house and gardens of Ham became the expression of supreme luxury and elegance in the time of Charles II. John Evelyn claimed it to be 'inferior to few of the best villas in Italy' and he knew most of them from first hand.[1] As a good gardener, he enthused about the 'parterres, flower gardens, orangeries, groves, avenues, courts, statues, perspectives, fountains, aviaries and all this at the banks of the sweetest river in the world.' The formal gardens are now in the process of being restored with lime trees and maples, poplars alternating with holly as the main surround. Hornbeam hedges supply the precise geometry of the inner paths. To the west lies another walled garden with roses, hollyhocks and exotic trees. Tea on such a lawn in such sun-drenched solitude is a welcome bonus. Yet another small garden stands to the east of the house with yew hedge, more hornbeams growing to create a leafy 'tunnel' and a silver flourish of santolina. Richmond and Ham are two sides of the coin of landscape gardening, both exquisite in their own way.

The Middlesex side of the river opposite Ham was lined with opulent villas, Marble Hill, Cambridge House, Twickenham Park, Mount Lebanon, York House, Orleans House and Pope's villa. Alexander Pope was the 'contriver' of the garden at Marble Hill which still keeps its black walnut, the largest in Britain. Fine gardens and exotic trees, waterfalls and statuary line the river bank. Pope invested the area with classical virtues, the harmony of man and nature in the direct imagery of Homer and Virgil. He contented himself with a mere five acres, suited to his own diminutive form. Whilst abhoring the strict formality of earlier years, he still sought a controlled conjunction of utility and naturalness. A school stands on the site of his estates, his famous grotto still surviving under the road.

The river is still 'sweet' as the tow-path lined with ash, willow, elder and hawthorn, leads south towards Teddington. Amongst the wayside flowers, Himalayan balsam grows in abundance. There is tansy going to seed but still keeping a powerful spicy smell. The bramble is still in flower and the bullfinches and chaffinches skim through the waste of Ham Common with kestrels floating above. Four cormorants sweep down the river from Syon towards the lowering sun. A small stone monolith announces the landward limit of the Port of London Authority in 1909 where the great willows have survived every variation of tide and flood. Then the river's calm assurance is rudely interrupted by locks and sluices and a footbridge leads over to Teddington.

There is a choice of routes here, either continuing along the tow-path to Kingston or crossing the river and taking a mile of road past the two churches of Teddington, old and new side by side, to reach the royal park of Bushy by the Teddington Gate, and be greeted by Christopher Wren's mile-long avenue of chestnut trees planted for William III. This is royal, not just two lines of trees but a phalanx marching in rows towards the Palace at Hampton. The storms of January, 1978 wreaked havoc in the park, tearing some trees by the roots, breaking others off at head height from the ground. One of the tragedies of the man-made landscapes is that many of the trees are now past their prime and are vulnerable to disease and storm. Formal Bushy may be, unlike Richmond, but it roars with deer. Both fallow and red roam in the park and make the level ground reverberate with their annual exertions. To the east lies the busier side of the park, so divert to the west and seek the deer by the Waterhouse Plantation and the Longford river. River is a mis-nomer for in Bushy even the water is tamed. In 1638, Charles I ordered the canalisation of nine miles of water to bring a constant supply into the park. Trapped by two warring stags and a bewildered herd of fifty hinds, I found myself hard by the Longford banks and wondered at its depth.

The Heron Pond, the Leg of Mutton Pond, the Long Water are all attractions to birds and Bushy, with its thousand wild acres is a nature reserve. Grey wagtails, sandpipers, redstarts, lapwings, great-crested grebes, even hoopoes and oyster catchers have been sighted in this green fastness. Formally 'a naked piece of ground' according to John Evelyn, it was planted with 'sweet rows of lime trees' all radiating from the Diana Fountain which was moved by Queen Anne from the gardens at Hampton. All this is the prelude to

Hampton, its outer wilderness a visual preparation for the inner pleasure grounds round the Tudor palace, the ultimate destination of a walk that began on a wasteland, traversed two deer parks and a river and ended with sunset over the sunken gardens.

Hampton was a monastic garden until Henry VIII acquired the estate from Cardinal Wolsey, a place of meditation and serenity. That sense of tranquillity is still present on an October evening in the privy garden or along the barge walk, the meadows on the Surrey side sloping down to the quiet river, the anglers wrapped in their private mystery. The Thames is still the genius of the place, the gardens its green consort. The well-drained gravelly soils gave Henry the healthful air he sought and he extended the park, taking in commons and meadows until 'the king's liege people were much diminished'. Many changes have been wrought since the Tudor enclosure. The gardens, like the palace, are an amalgam of many reigns, of many styles, from monastic simplicity to Tudor formality, from Carolingian splendour to Georgian romanticism.

Charles II, inspired by memories of Versailles, worked on the grand scale and planned the 'crow's foot' of paths and lawns to the east of the house, leading to the Long Water. William of Orange spent much time at the Court refashioning the grounds and building the great terrace walk by the river. Between terrace and gardens Jean Tijou's superb screen of wrought iron made a barrier that framed rather than impeded the open view beyond. The famous maze was contrived by Henry Wise in the time of Queen Anne, and George London planted exotic trees brought to Hampton by plant hunters from every corner of the known world.

In the eighteenth century Capability Brown became Surveyor to His Majesty's Gardens and Waters but made very few changes to the general pattern 'out of respect to himself and his profession'.[2] Hampton was fine enough already. In his time, the black Hambro vine was brought as a cutting from Valentine's Park in Essex. The knobbly pale stump, seven feet in girth, is still full of life, witness the arcade of foliage along the glass roof and the bunches of grapes still hanging in October long after the main picking.

The Pond Garden and the Knot Garden are full of late summer colour planted with geometric precision, fed since the early seventeenth century with canal water. So the royal garden has evolved, reflecting the passage of time and fashion until it was finally opened to the public pleasure by Queen Victoria in 1838.

To the east of the house, the sun throws long shadows across the lawns, picking out the red berries of the clipped yews like jewels in a medieval embroidery, the grass like an emerald green back-cloth. The umbrella shape of the topiary makes the perfect shelter in a sudden heavy shower and three moorhen waddle over from the Long Water to join me. Coots gather in the water and hoot their challenges, running over the surface in violent chase, heads down, tail feathers raised like rudders, then lay back and fight each other beak and claw. Then they dip under the water in a convulsion of spray until the vanquished accepts defeat and takes refuge on the far bank. A heron, royal bird, rises from the bank and flaps with easy wing-beat towards Kingston, scarcely diverted from its direct course by the attentions of a black-backed gull which attacks it from above.

I follow the heron's flight through the darkening park back to the Kingston Gate where the sheep are grazing in their enclosure. Above, the gulls are drifting in their thousands, sometimes in V-formations, sometimes line abreast, only just discernible in the greying sky, always westwards to their roost on the Thames reser-voirs.

Hyde Park
O Caldecott 82

11
RESIDENT
BIRDS

The farmer was proud of his black sheep. By crossing the ancient breed of Jacob's sheep with Suffolks, he had produced completely black lambs. They were his hobby, but his livelihood depended on cattle, and it was time to feed them. He jumped on the tractor and we crunched through the icy puddles along the farm track, past the remnants of the original medieval moat hidden amongst the trees to the south of Downs Barn Farm, to the big pasture at the far end of the lane where the young Hereford bull was charging around playfully amongst a herd of Friesian cows. They all came lumbering after the tractor and formed a long line as the hay bales were thrown off the cart. There seemed to be plenty of bite left on the long grass after a wet autumn but there was little nutritional value in it so the additional hay was necessary to maintain the milk yield. The cattle devoured it eagerly, steam rising from their mouths in the frosty air. Large flocks of gulls and starlings wheeled about the field. A flock of long-tailed tits flickered along the hedgerow and two kestrels called to each other with high, thin voices. Then yellowhammers passed by and a solitary bright bullfinch. 'Interested in birds?' asked the farmer. 'Very', I said. 'Have you seen the herons?' he waved towards a small stream trickling through the wet pastures. I followed his invitation and splodged down to the heron territory not only to encounter herons but a whole galaxy of birds. To the south was the industrial skyline of Southall and, to the north, the incessant traffic of Western Avenue and the comparative calm of Northolt Airport.

Within a hundred yards of the frenzy of cars, I encountered a

143

siege of herons, flapping lazily in the sky, a walk of snipe zig-
zagging from cover with cries of alarm, a charm of goldfinches
feeding on seed-heads, an exaltation of larks rising in the morning
air and a tiding of magpies. One for sorrow, two for joy. So the
'tidings' run, up to 'ten for the devil's own self' but there were no
less than twenty-five magpies gathered by the spinney and I don't
know what tidings that number holds in store. It always seems to be
black birds that are associated with omens, blackbird, rook, crow,
raven, magpie, just right for the day after Hallowe'en. Does the
'mag' of magpie really have the same root as Margaret? Magpies
they are called in some places, haggisters in others. Speculating on
such mysteries, I saw a very large thrush with grey head and
reddish breast, alight on a hawthorn bush only twenty yards from a
man selling bags of potatoes from the roadside. It was the first
fieldfare of the winter arriving from the Baltic for our milder climes,
and a feast of berries.

Then I saw the birds I had really come to find. Amongst the
gulls and starlings were the lapwings, dozens and dozens of them.
They took off at my approach, crests down and floated over the dual
carriageway into the sanctuary of Northolt airport, one of their
favourite collecting grounds for the autumn congregation. Their
mournful 'peewit' cries were more in keeping with lonely marshes
than the west pastures of Hillingdon Borough. What group name
suits a flock of hundreds of lapwings? 'Deceit' has been used since
medieval times. 'The false lapwing, ful of trecherye' said *The Parle-
ment of Foules*. The 'deceit' is presumably derived from the bird's
cunning in feigning injury to lead intruders away from nesting sites.

The lapwing has been driven further and further from the
centre of London by the growth of the suburbs, the loss of open
farmland and the drainage of wet pastures. It prefers large fields and
fallow grounds where it can feed on insects, especially leatherjackets. The farmer's friend, it cleans the ground and is especially active
as the ground thaws out increasing grub activity. It 'gapes' for its
food, thrusting the long bill into the ground and opening it to find
the insect larvae. It has deserted many of its traditional breeding
grounds but still returns for the winter flocking, and there are few
places better than Northolt to see it. The sanctuary of the aerodrome
gives it a security that enables you to approach so closely that you
can see the rich markings, rich red patches and the whole elegant

144

stance which earns the nickname of 'the French maid'.

The lapwing still breeds along the more rural watercourses on the fringes of London and in recent years it has been recorded once again in the very heart in the wastelands of Surrey Docks. Other notable areas for flocking are the large fields at the foot of the North Downs escarpment and at Beddington in the vicinity of the sewage works.

Flocking is a feature of many species of birds and November one of the most rewarding months. A hard winter and frozen ground often drives them further afield though they will be seen again as the ground thaws in the early Spring. If the lapwing is a bird of the rural fringes, the starling is a species that has adapted successfully to the urban heart and its flocking can be studied as well in Leicester Square as in Northolt. I have watched their movements for many years now in a south London suburb. On a typical November day the first starling swept across the tree tops towards my window at almost one hour before sunset. It flew very fast, very straight, so straight that it was only at the last moment that the bird seemed to climb enough to clear the house top. A minute later ten more starlings passed overhead in a group, moving with short bursts of wing beats and long glides, occasionally veering into the wind but always maintaining the general direction towards the north-west. In the next five minutes, twenty-three birds, then fourteen. For the next hour the procession continued along the flight-path, in numbers varying from single birds to groups of twenty or more. As it grew darker, the birds were more difficult to pick out against the trees, so low did they fly. A flock of gulls drifted over in the same general direction but at much greater height. And still the starlings came. They were gathering in four plane trees nearby where they met with another flight line from the east over Shooters Hill. Transferring my vantage point to the avenue I watched them sweep in, circle briefly and then join the flock on the branches, often dislodging the dying leaves. A murmuration of starlings was not the word I would have used for that cacophony of sound. It was just as if a great reunion was taking place and everyone had the news of the day to exchange. As more birds arrived, the flock spilt over on to other trees the avenue. I estimated about five hundred starlings in the group making a noise loud enough to be heard above the rush-hour traffic nearby when suddenly, five minutes before sunset, there was a complete silence followed by a rush of wings as the whole flock took off for the last leg of their daily journey towards central London. One or two birds were left behind and some stragglers came along a few minutes later circled the trees twice and then continued their flight.

The culmination of the starlings' journey is one of the great sights of London. Just before sunset in St James's Park, the birds start arriving and often drop down for a while on to the trees on the island in the lake. Another time they circle, change direction and head straight for Trafalgar Square. The pattern varies slightly. Flocks from all points of the compass gather above Northumberland Avenue high above the office blocks of the Ministry of Defence and the Ministry of Agriculture, Food and Fishing, forming and reforming, wheeling and rising.

Some of them settle amongst the pigeons already roosting on the ledges of the buildings, on cornice and coping. Others drop to the trees along the Embankment Gardens. Then the whole flock rises again and sweeps towards Trafalgar Square. Nelson is plastered with starlings, while the pigeons huddle around the plinth. Then the final enormous commotion as the main bulk of the birds reach the foot of Charing Cross Road making even the earnest pleasure seekers in the bright lights below look up with a sense of wonder. One paper stall owner who had seen it all for many years, dusk after dusk, said to me knowingly, 'And there's only one leader'. As he said it the birds flew in a great mass between the buildings along Irving Street into the plane trees of Leicester Square, flock after flock seeking the heart of London's 'heat island'. There is just a hint of fear as well as wonder in such a sight. While the crowds sauntered around the pedestrian ways that have made the Square a much more civilised place, the birds shouted and chattered as the roost filled up. Estimates of as many as 50,000 birds have been made in such a roost. I mentioned this to the paper stall man and he repeated that there was only one leader. I spent the next hour listening to the birds, watching them move from tree to tree, wondering what control mechanism existed in such a mighty gathering.

At least thirteen of these flight-paths have been observed around London with birds moving in from the suburbs to the central roosts, some birds travelling from as far as fourteen miles out. I have watched the starlings in the Cray Valley on the outskirts of south-east London fifteen miles from Trafalgar Square. A grouping took place towards sunset near Foots Cray church then the birds flew off in the opposite direction, away from the suburbs towards the Darent Valley. In that area, near Eynsford, is one of the biggest winter roosts I have ever seen, but a mixed roost, not just of starlings. Not all starlings join the major roosts. Some form small local roosts and others remain in comparative isolation. The central roosts are believed to be composed of local birds, the regulars as it were and not of the many starlings which move in from the continent for the winter.

The starling rather than the sparrow strikes me as being the classic urban bird and not just because of its commuting patterns in reverse. Garrulous, gregarious, its head feathers sometimes have the look of greased down hair. It even seems to run as if it has its hands in its pockets, a confident urban bird full of good cheer and banter and capable of the most extraordinary mimicry with a repertoire of squeaks, whistles, trills and like noises piped from the rooftops. Even when a flock of a hundred or more feed in the morning outside my window they do it with pattern and purpose, each to his own space, always moving on, ready for trouble, wary yet at home in the group. They really work their territory, systematically digging. A lawn after their visit is pock-marked with holes. Completely adapted to the city yet the bird is remarkably independent of man.

The London roosts have been recorded since the end of the last century with estimates of anything between three million and seven million resident birds. Despite the impression that some starlings give of being wise old birds, their mortality rate is just about 50 per cent with a typical adult life of something under two years though some birds are known to have lived for up to sixteen years.

As the landscape becomes more barren so we become more aware of birds. The summer migrants have gone and the winter visitors not fully in evidence so we are left with the regulars so to speak. The observations have a different quality. It's as if the birds are drawn by the comparative warmth of London, the chance of augmenting their usual food with household pickings. It's an inbetween time. Walking across my local heath one miserable November day after copious overnight rain, I noted an unusual

147

succession of sightings. A jack-snipe more at home on the marshes suddenly took off from a flock of starlings and flew abreast of the cars on the main road. It left the cars standing with its swift flight. Then amongst the gulls, getting more and more numerous with each day was a flock of about fifty pied wagtails working over a wet hollow with short stuttering runs, tails dipping. These birds are widespread in London, even as a breeding species, but I seldom see as many at one time. They look like masked bandits with their black and white facial markings.

There was a commotion up above, a host of sparrows mobbing a kestrel, which had no difficulty at all in evading their attention with easy turns, climbs and changes of speed. The kestrel is probably London's most numerous bird of prey which has adapted itself to the man-made cliffs of tall buildings, for its nesting sites. Its food in the inner area is largely of house-sparrows, hence the attention of the sparrow mob. In the outer commons and spaces its diet includes a larger proportion of rodents. It is a familiar sight hovering above main roads, possibly using the updraughts of warmer air from hard surfaces. Its only rival as an urbanised bird-of-prey is the tawny owl which had taken up its winter station in the plane tree outside my house and fills the rooms with its melancholy calls. In the larger open spaces and commons the tawny owl feeds largely on a diet of rodents, but it has moved into the inner parks where it preys on other birds, especially the sparrow, thrush, starling and even the feral pigeon.

Leaving the open heath and turning into the park, I was in the more familiar morning territory of blackbird and thrush, lined up along the grass as still and wary as sentries. Heads dip, a short run, a turn of the head, a dig into the wet grass. Then two approached too close and they spiralled into the air, breast to breast, beak to sharp beak, wings fluttering wildly, up and down until one retreated. A native of woodland, copse and hedgerow, the blackbird has adapted so successfully to urban living that it is now the fourth most numerous breeding bird in London, having had, in this century, something of a population explosion. The ornithologists now feel it has reached its optimum population. It has a wide range of diet, from worms and insects to garden scraps, bread, fat, anything. Yet it always seems to be a bird of the wild, flashing across the garden in rapid flight, freezing on the fence, clucking its constant challenge and warning, amongst the last to come down for the morning breadcrumbs and the first to take to flight when the back-door opens. One of the sounds I always associate with the blackbird, as with the thrush, is the noise of dry leaves being turned over. A bird that seems to run as much as it flies, it is always on patrol, amongst the last to roost and the first up in the dawning. The song thrush is as widespread as the blackbird but does not seem to have adopted its catholic feeding habits, depending still on worms and snails. Even quicker to flight from its bold, upright stance, it needs tree cover and bushes for its comfort.

Then came the carrion crow, king of all it surveyed, proceeding with a slow but deliberate gait and an occasional hop to scatter the starlings and sparrows and any other rival in reach to gather the tit-bits of the morning. W.H. Hudson called the crow the 'grandest wild bird left to us in the metropolis' but its depredations may account for the decline of other birds, such as the lapwing and even the sparrow, though the losses have also been blamed on the magpie. Carrion always seems an ugly word but the crow is a great bread eater and investigates every paper bag and scrap left behind by the park visitors. It is at home in all the parks and nests even in the inner parks with the exception of St James's where it is only recorded as being 'observed' on the latest record. You only appreciate its size when it hobbles amongst the other birds. The carrion crow is a constant menace to the ducklings that abound in the same parks but Hudson felt that a few losses thereby was no great harm. He scorned the idea of turning London parks into what he called 'poultry farms'.

The grasslands of garden lawn, playing field, park and common are not the only feeding grounds for the wintering birds. They turn their attention to the hedgerows and bushes crammed with berries. There are many exotica available now like the cotoneaster and the many types of viburnum that give additional sustenance, but the dominant species is the hawthorn. Left alone, the hawthorn can grow into a substantial tree, but it is most familiar as a hedgerow plant. The words hedge and haw may be related, the old English haga. Also known as the quick, the very essence of life, the hawthorn leaf may be seen curling out of the mouth of Jack-in-the-Green, the spirit of vegetation. I read a story once that the hawthorn flower preserved the smell of London's plague! But it is the fruit in

November that is so vital. It has a variety of names, aggle, agog, hipperty haw. It is just about the most tolerant plant of all, colonising the urban wastes, able to withstand human pressures. There is a patch of waste I pass on the way to work where the hawthorns and silver birches have grown into a scrubland, and, in their shelter, other plants are thriving. This natural regeneration is so much more effective than plant-a-tree campaigns. We need more hedges, more areas of untended scrub. Let the wild return in the unwanted corners of the city. The birds enjoy them. At a time when we are losing something like two thousand miles of hedgerow every year in farming areas, the city can help to redress the balance. The trees that smothered my suburban garden were all the result of seedlings that a passing bird had deposited in the stiff clay.

The hawthorn is the main constituent plant of the hedges in the London area whether on the 300-year-old hedgerows of Enfield Chase, or 200-year-old enclosures of Bromley Common or the medieval boundaries on Coulsdon Down. There could be few more rewarding ways of spending November than hunting the hedgerows. That's where the berries will be. That's where the birds will be. And other creatures using the hedges as their highways from space to space. On Bromley Common, for example, which was enclosed in about 1812, the hawthorn dominates. But over a thirty-yard stretch another plant comes in, either holly or elder or sycamore and, in one place, oak. Two species in thirty yards gives a hedge of between one and two hundred years which fits nicely with the known documentary evidence.

In the Hainault area the forest was divided up into farms after 1851 and there we find the hawthorn dominant and often the only hedgerow species. On the Enfield Chase, disafforested and divided up into hedged fields three centuries ago, the hawthorn has been joined by oak and elder. So a close view of hedges supplies a new clue in the history of London's countryside. I find myself wandering around London looking for hedges. Going south-east they begin at Bromley Common or at Mottingham. Going north-east they start close by the A12 at Aldborough Hatch. On the Great North Road, you find them close to the Mill Hill roundabout. On the west way towards Northolt, the first hedgerows appear soon after the industrial estates of Park Royal. There is even a hedge surviving along the centre of the dual carriageway. On such a section with ruined elms overgrown with ivy, I once saw a dozen or more red admiral butter-flies feeding on the pollen of ivy amidst the swarm of flies and wasps, all making the most of the year's last supply. The ivy comes into its own when all else is on the wane. Not only does it give food but shelter. It can grow for a hundred years and produce a dark world of its own amongst the woody stems and abundant evergreen foliage.

The nearest hedge I know to the starling's chosen centre of London at Leicester Square is in Green Park, a good beech hedge. There's a fine hawthorn hedge, too, in Hyde Park. But many of the garden hedges in inner London turn their backs on the hawthorn and adopt the privet. Clipped too strongly, the privet loses much of its sweet-smelling white blossom and its potential crop of black berries in autumn. Many birds eat the berries and avoid the hard seeds. Pruning the privet was always my juvenile job and a tricky one. The strong stems had a habit of escaping the shears making the Sunday afternoon chore seem longer and longer. I have had a higher regard for the privet since seeing it growing wild on the chalk country of the North Downs and especially since I found that it was related to the olive. My garden hedge brought back memories of Greece as I clipped it in the late summer. Almost an evergreen, in that it bears some leaves most of the year, the bush nevertheless does shed it lanceolate leaves by the Spring. It has been known as a garden hedge since the sixteenth century at least and has been given a variety of names such as blacktops, privy and primprint. I always thought the name had some relationship to private, hence the privy garden but evidently there is no such connection, the word privet being of obscure origin. Its Latin name *liguistrum* comes from *ligo*, to bind, the stems being used to bind up bundles.

Privet is seen at its best in a mixed hedgerow such as those incomparable boundaries that march along the edges of Coulsdon Down and the Happy Valley, full of berries of every colour and leaves of hues that defy description. One such November morning waking with clear sunlight put summer to shame, the air soon filled with lark song. A magpie was tearing at the corpse of a rabbit and the finches were scurrying through the hedges. The rich, red berry of guelder rose was stripped and the stem turned back like a flower. The elders were nearly all taken and the dogwood berries looked like squashed currants. The buckthorn berries were swelling up and the spindle, loveliest of all, beginning to ripen, fat four-sectioned pink cases containing the four hard orange seeds, the leaves bronze and red, curling and falling to the ground. A kestrel hovered above a noisy congregation of starlings while the goldfinches turned their attention to the seed heads of knapweed even though some of the flower heads were still in bloom. An elderly couple sitting by one of the picnic tables declared that Coulsdon in November was better than Spain had been in August. What a morning that was to wander along the hedgerows counting the species and observing their bounty of berries, hawthorn, holly, privet, wayfaring tree, hazel, oak, dogwood, ash, maple, cherry, elm. In contrast there is a clipped hedge that runs straight across the Happy Valley, all hawthorn with ash trees growing out of it and dogwood just colonising, a mere two hundred years old, a landscape stripling compared with the venerable ancients of the upper slopes.

Another area of interesting hedgerows, containing many of the species associated with chalk country, such as the dogwood, the hazel and the wayfaring tree is at Selsdon. This part of the Borough of Croydon is of comparatively recent growth, new housing biting into the woodland and the pastures but there is one woodland which is jealously guarded, together with its ancient hedgerows and fields and that is the Selsdon Bird Sanctuary, maintained by the local borough and the National Trust.

Only a half mile to the south from the Selsdon sanctuary is Farleigh Green. Just within the London bounds, this is an almost entirely rural survival, a scrubby green dotted by hawthorns, bounded by a ditch and a broad shaw of trees, backed by farmland with a pub at one end and a farm and stables at the other. The little Norman church lies to the east by footpath, alongside its Court Farm. This type of settlement, a church, a Court house and farm is typical of Surrey and Kent in manorial estates that belonged to the church, in this case, the Bishop of Rochester.

Standing in the middle of Farleigh Green with London seeming a landscape away I recalled another green that I had seen from the unusual vantage point of a motorway flyover on the way out west to Northolt and the lapwings. There within a stone's throw of the speeding traffic was the classical facade of St Mary's on Paddington Green. John Rocque's map of London, compiled just over two hundred years ago showed Paddington on the rural fringes of the built-up area, just about the same situation that Farleigh occupies today. If Green Belt restrictions mean anything, Farleigh will never be overtaken by the building mania as Paddington has. Surrounded by towering blocks, a children's hospital and just one or two buildings that do not offend the eye, the green abuts on to the extensive churchyard lined with plane trees and wire fences which are brutally urban. I looked for pretty little Polly Perkins of the traditional ditty, as sweet as a butterfly and proud as a queen, and found instead a statue of Sarah Siddons, the actress. Her tomb, covered with ornate ironwork, stands neglected in the churchyard. The survival of the ancient village greens in London is a feature of its topography, though, in Paddington's case, a more rustic atmosphere is to be found north of the green along the fine houses of St Mary's Terrace and Park Place to the boat basin of Little Venice, with lock cottage that would not be out of place in rural Hertfordshire. Cottage, boats brightly painted, mallard in abundance, tree-lined streets, houses set in greenery, Little Venice almost achieves the atmosphere that the old village might have had before new roads and new buildings change it for ever.

Greens bearing the most rural of names are found in the most unexpected places, such as Shepherd's Bush Green, once a hamlet of Hammersmith and now in effect a grand traffic island. Once it was a swampy waste surrounded by a ditch and known as Gagglegoose Green. Speculation about the shepherd's bush seems to agree it was a venerable hawthorn used by shepherds as a watchbox. They leaned against it, sat on it so often that it was worn smooth. The old green was 'improved', that is to say tidied up, drained, planted with trees, the usual planes, and made into a public open space in 1871. To the south is another long straggling green called Brook Green, a mere five acres shaped like a dart with another theatrical memory, for Henry Irving once lived by its side. In the same vicinity, once belonging to the manor Fulham, is Parson's Green, famed for its probable association with fair Rosamund, favourite of Edward III. She had rural bowers in Kent, too. Nearby are the fourteen acres of Eel Brook Common, once having the more memorable name of Hellbrook Common. These spaces all date from the time when the heart of Fulham was the bishop's palace by the Thames and the rest was pasture, orchard and market garden.

There are notable 'greens' in the congested urbanity of the East End such as Stepney Green, a patch of green and some hawthorn hedgerow at the junction with Whitehorse Lane. The prospect improves round the corner towards Mile End, with a recognisable triangle of land and a fine tree-lined walkway by the buildings, the Jewish hospital and a handful of Queen Anne houses. The East End was already becoming an industrial area, with craft workshops in the time of Queen Anne but the fields were close to the green then. Recent clearance of poorer housing has left new areas of grass around the site of the old green. But the best open space at Stepney is by the church of St George, a large impressive church and church-yard containing a variety of trees, including a mulberry. This churchyard, with its children's playground, was one of the first to be dedicated as a public open-space, in 1876. An inscription by the door of the church is a remarkable reflection of the growth of London for it reads that sixty-six more parishes have been carved out of the once great parish of St George.

A short walk away to the north, across the broad, tree-lined Mile End Road and the statue of William Booth, is another church-yard as the centre piece of an important open space with pubs and streets with rural names like Three Colts Lane. Bethnal Green, once part of the common waste of Stepney was purchased in 1667 to be preserved as the Poor's Lands, expressly 'for the prevention of any new buildings thereon'. The new museum took four and a half acres in 1968 and the high price of land encouraged the trustees to sell more. Strong opposition from local people, the newly formed LCC and the Metropolitan Gardens Association saved what was left of the orchards, paddock and kitchen gardens. They were laid out afresh as a public space. On the wall of the museum facing the open space is a frieze of countryside activities, ploughing, hoeing, train-ing trees, mowing, hay-making, shearing sheep, may flowers, wheat harvest, hopping, picking apples, fishing, buying beasts, the dairy, almost a country year. Pepys recalled 'the greatest quantities of strawberries I ever saw, and good'.

The Saxons called the month Blodmonarth, the month of sac-rifices and it still remains the month of ritual for Londoners. Some of the rituals are deep in our past, some of recent invention yet they all seem to combine in a folk memory of fire and smoke and the cleansing of the year before the winter, the dead half of the country year. In the City of Westminster, the Guy burns within sight of the building he tried to destroy by fire and gunpowder. A week later

154

Whitehall rings to the sounds of martial music, the last post and the celebration of the dead, the pavements red with poppies. In the other more ancient city, the Lord Mayor rides in a golden carriage on the second Saturday in the month. It may be pure coincidence that such ceremonies and celebrations occur at the very time of the year when, in our Celtic past, the dead, too, were celebrated, with fire. Frazer has suggested a hallowe'en link with tradition even older than the Saxons, back beyond to the Britons, the Celtic people with a pastoral tradition, a year based on the movement of livestock, with two turning points, 1 May and 1 November. Such speculation recalls London's Celtic past, a London older than the Roman Londinium. What of the gods, Gog and Magog who still stand in the Guildhall? What of King Lud, whose gate is remembered? More certainly even a place name like Penge in the southern hilly suburbs has a name that contains two Celtic elements, pen, the spur of land, coat, the woodland. How old is the ceremony that used to take place at Hainault Forest on 11 November when at midnight the eldest man present would drive an axe into the branch of an old oak tree? Ritual has a habit of perpetuating itself in new disguises. Even the word Guy is linked with the 'guisers' of more ancient ceremony.

Guy himself gains more variety every year. At Lambeth, just across from Parliament, he stands in the High Street, life-sized, clad in complete fireman's uniform. At Stepney Green he is a stuffed doll slumped on a park seat on a bright morning of 6 November only a firecracker's jump away from the debris of last night's fire. The fallen boughs and branches from the commons that were once the essential winter fuel for cottager and commoner have found a new use. In John Stow's London three hundred years ago bonfires were lit 'for the amity of neighbours' and also, he added, 'for the virtue that a great fire hath to purge the infection of the air.' There is something satisfying about a good burn-up though the fire brigade would not agree. The rubbish from the gardens, the pruning, the dead flowers, all symbolise the last of summer, making the place ship-shape before the winter. November's fires end the chapter that began with May Day's garlands and ritual tree from the greenwood. The city invents new reasons but the basic rhythms of the countryside supply the underlying causes.

155

Yew Tree
St Mary the Virgin
Downe

12
ALL THAT IS GREEN

In the first days of the last month the sights and smells of the countryside come to town and so do the countrymen, with their ruddy faces and tweedy clothes, fresh from the northern fells and the wide fields of the eastern plains all converging on the great barn of the exhibition hall way out west at Earls Court. The Smithfield Show is on again and the supreme champion will be crowned king for a year. The agricultural show still bears the name of its original venue close to Smithfield by the City's walls, in Wotton's Livery Stables in Dolphin Yard to be exact, where it first met in 1799, at a time when agricultural improvement was all the rage. Then it moved to the horse bazaar in Baker Street before moving in the 1860s to the Agricultural Hall near Islington Green, traditional centre of the droving trade. My father was brought up within earshot of the cattle ring and knew his livestock well as a boy before moving on to flowers, fruit and vegetables in 'the Garden' in the Duke of Bedford's piazza. The building still stands, a vast empty space waiting for a new destiny whilst the cattle and the sheep and the pigs and the countrymen moved on after the Second World War to the new Exhibition Hall at Earls Court.

You soon realise what has happened to modern farming. The whole ground floor is packed with gleaming machines, tractors, combine harvesters, hay balers, fork-lift trucks, potato pickers, chemical sprayers with the ambitious young grappling with the steering and the gears in the mercifully stationary monsters. Gents in smart suits stand by with ready advice and the hope of a sale. At the far end is the smell of cattle, the lumbering beasts standing in

157

rows of patience. Some give up and lie down, nostrils steaming, eyes wary. The supreme champion of the year stands in his glass cage, oblivious focus of admiring eyes. The great bull is more concerned with the hay liberally strewn beneath his feet. Two centuries ago it was the Sussex Red and the Hereford bull, Durham shorthorn, the Devon red and other regional breeds. Today the traditional colours have been supplanted by the dun colours of imported breeds, the Charolais, the Limousin, the Simmenthal. Mysterious equations appear above the pens, Simmenthal cross Friesian and Shorthorn cross Aberdeen Angus. The supreme champion bears a name as undignified as Thingummyjig but he looks magnificent, more powerful than the greatest of the machines.

Upstairs, tucked away behind the chemicals and the seed displays are the pigs and the sheep. The sheep breeds have reassuringly familiar names like Cheviot and Scottish Blackface, Southdown and Romney, though even here the unusual and the exotic make their appearance. Ancient breeds appear, the black St Kilda and the four-horned Jacob, and local breeds like the Whitefaced Woodland and the Leicester Longwool with fleece as coarse as a knitted jersey. The layman's eye runs over the tight-clipped beauties, as pampered and prepared as film stars, and wonders what qualities gave this one first prize and that one a mere recommend. The sheep seem in a perpetual state of agitation but the pigs have ceased to bother and lie out flat in magnificent relaxation, fresh pink bodies trembling and eyes twitching in perpetual dreams. There are the Landrace and the saddlebacks, the Hampshires with white belts sleeping out the week-long chore, in unaccustomed pens and noise.

The loudspeaker breaks out with scarce concealed irritation calling the young farmers into the ring and they gaze in commanded silence at the fresh sides of meat, judging quality and quantity, and dream of a fleeting fame when they return home to the farm. Walking the wet pastures around Harefield, or trudging the downs behind Keston, it is still possible to view the farm animals as yet one more visual ingredient of the eternal countryside. Here, rubbing shoulders with the 100,000 visitors and the gleaming booths of new farm wares, the illusion goes and the animals are seen as just one part, albeit the essential part, of an industry, the production of food. For a moment the countryside becomes a factory floor, the beasts merely part of the conveyor belt of food production to feed London's rapacious market. Then a man scratches the nose of a Hereford steer and the brute comes to life, its smells, its sounds, its very presence evocative of open fields and lush meadows and the wind rolling down from the hills. It is still an industry with a difference. It is still a conjunction of man and his countryside and, for some of the shepherds and the cattlemen, it's their first visit to the city and they look just a little uncomfortable.

I leave the great show and thread my way along the streets throbbing with the season's business and there is a stall decked out with greenery for sale. There is holly, of course, and mistletoe probably from France. Then there is the fresh foliage of cypress, splayed out like palms and the stiff pointed leaves of butcher's broom smothered with silver paint. That plant has an odd link with the Smithfield Show for it may have gained its name from the custom of butchers decorating their Christmas sirloins with its twigs and red berries. It is not a common plant in the London area but it appears in the Queen's garden at Kew and small patches occur in areas of oak woodland such as Epping and Shooters Hill. The ancient herbalists granted it the quality of opening and cleansing, a useful attribute after the Christmas excess. Alongside the butcher's broom and similarly silvered was the teasel, perhaps the most startling of the floral seedheads, at its most magnificent in late summer rimmed with purple flowers, besieged by peacock butterflies. The ivy is the surest symbol of winter's defeat for its berries are just filling out into fat purple clusters and its qualities of protection from ill and evil were as revered as those of the holly itself.

The next stall was devoted to the Christmas trees themselves. Ten of them standing end to end would just match the height of the Trafalgar Square spruce. They are the babies, a mere ten or twenty years in the growing, the thinnings of the forest plantations. There is no problem in the picking. You could have your own nursery in the back garden though they do not like a heavy clay soil. Even so there are plenty of well-drained soils in London where they would flourish. Put them five feet apart and you can grow nearly a hundred of these midgets in the same space a mature oak would need. That, of course, is one of the reasons for their popularity with the timber trade. They grow fast and straight and true and have a quick return, a market within a dozen years or so. The spruce has long reached its

159

maturity when the oak tree is a mere stripling.

The name of the spruce is related to Prussia, one of its original homelands, where the needles were used to flavour a special beer and its bark made a type of leather. It was introduced to England as early as 1548. The larch followed close on its heels in the early years of the seventeenth century. The European larch has been ousted in the affection of foresters by the Japanese larch, introduced in 1861 and by various hybrids which are resistant to disease. All these species and many more can be seen in plantations within the London boundary, especially at Joyden's Wood near Bexley and in the High Elms estate near Bromley. The woodland rides offer many pleasures in December days, bramble leaves scarlet, their spiky branches carrying fruit that will never ripen. Hazel and whitebeam are already showing the tentative buds of red and yellow that anticipate a new season of growing. The last yellowing needles of larch are stiff with frost. As cold damp air drifts in from the northeast the icy halo round the last leaves of autumn seems to grow as you watch. In a burnt area the fat fleshy leaves of rhododendron are flourishing, a plant that has naturalised so successfully that it competes with oak and birch seedlings for new territories to colonise.

The solemn columns of Lodgepole and Corsican pines stand guard behind the last heather patches of the old heathland and, on the summits, are the twisted, tufty tops of the Scots pine, our only native conifer. Then there are the occasional giants, the American redwoods with their fibrous, rufus barks that became popular in the 1850s in public parks and private gardens and, as the Wellingtonia, were given the name of a giant amongst men. Some of them have grown a hundred feet in a hundred years and still have two thousand years to go to reach their full maturity.

With such abundant greenery available, Londoners today can more than emulate the customs of their Tudor forebears as recorded by John Stow. 'Against the feast of Christmas every man's house, as also the parish churches, were decked out with holm, ivy, bays and whatsoever the season of the year afforded to be green.' It is likely that Stow had the holly in mind when he wrote of the 'holm' though the holm oak or ilex, a native of the Mediterranean, would have been known to him, having been introduced into England by the time of his *Survey of London*.[1] In many London parks it is as familiar as the holly itself, growing into a fine tree with a regular canopy of glossy spiky leaves. Its acorns are much prized by pigeons for winter food. Sometimes the birds pick the acorns from their cups or take the easier course of snapping the twigs and sampling the fat seeds at their leisure on the ground. The squirrels, more dexterous at ground level, sprint in to grab the prize and make off to bury it in some private cache in the flower beds.

The holm can never replace the holly in our affections, for the native tree is the perfect symbol of Christmas, the spiky leaves relating to the crown of thorns and the berries like drops of blood. It was used to defend the houses against lightning and witchcraft and goblins, even in Roman times. Being tolerant of shade it forms much of the under-storey of London's oak woodlands and in parklands many variegated forms have been developed, with delicate yellow edges to the leaves, some even with yellow berries. Many birds feed on the berries, especially the thrushes.

Another evergreen not mentioned specifically by Stow yet known to the Tudors was the box, a native tree of the chalklands that was doomed to be clipped into fantastic shapes and trim boundary hedges. Perhaps it found no favour as a household decoration because it was reputed to smell like cats. Seldom reaching great stature, the box suffers from brittle boughs that fall in high winds yet its wood is nearly as tough as that of the holly and much prized for special turnery, for boxes, rulers and wood engraving blocks. Its delicate sprays of tiny oval leaves and small white flowers forming early in the winter are as likely to be seen in London gardens as in its native habitat on the North Downs where it is now a rare tree.

If all London is now an arboretum, Kew is the microcosm. Many of the trees that are now such a familiar part of our city landscape began at Kew, from seeds brought from every corner of the world by exploring botanists. The wonder of winter greenery starts as soon as you leave the ducks on the frozen pond by the Victoria Gate and walk beyond the Palm House. Here the holly is clipped into hedgerows and topiary work and the avenue towards the river is lined with holm oaks. The barren trees, set against such a dark green blackcloth, are as visually exciting as the evergreens. The weeping ash bangs its delicate fretwork of bough, twig, and seed clusters against the sky. The Lucombe oak, a gardener's hybrid, still holds its leaves, yellowing and turning. All the acorns are gone, from both oak and ilex torn from their cups by the pigeons and squirrels. The avenue leads to the lake, dug out in the nineteenth century, its gravels used to surface the paths. Most of the wildfowl collection fell to a fox when the water was frozen during the 1976 winter but already other birds are making themselves at home, Canada geese, tufted duck and mallard. By the side of the lake is the main area of conifers, planted not in rows but in the tradition of English parklands so that they achieve a semi-natural setting. There are Chilean pines and Black pines in abundance, cedars and juniper and spruce and Douglas fir, redwoods and thuja, each tree dominating a small part of the total composition but never exclusively, never dull. Fortunately for the layman, like myself, the trees are generally labelled so that the pleasure of their appearance can be heightened by knowing what they are, and what exotic countryside was their homeland.

All the exotic shapes of trees and buildings, and gazebo, the pagoda and temple, the work of Sir William Chambers in the eighteenth century are nearly forgotten when you enter the Queen's cottage grounds, named after Queen Charlotte. Here is a piece of old England devoted to the entirely native plants, oak, beech, hornbeam, holly and yew with pheasants and rabbits shuffling through the leaf fall and looking for tit-bits. Set alongside the river, this part of Kew gives as good an idea as anything in London of what the Thames and its countryside must have been, before the fashion for riverside villas and palaces, before even the plough and the pasture. Hudson regarded this corner as one of the best bird sanctuaries in London and dreaded the clearing-up process that followed it becoming public in 1898. He feared that some of the forty-nine species of birds he recorded here would leave the area. At the last count, there were at least seventy-nine species of bird known here, including no less than forty-two species staying to breed. Moving northwards along the river to the focus of Syon Vista, the view opens out over the Thames and the mansion at Syon capped by the stiff-tailed lion, heraldic symbol of the Percy family, the Dukes of Northumberland. Across the river in a bare willow tree, twelve cormorants roost, as happily as if they were on Northumberland's wide-swept cliffs.

Along the riverside avenue there is the oak collection including evergreen species. Parallel with the avenue is another touch of Northumberland for the Rhododendron Dell is one of the few remnants of the work of Capability Brown, the renowned landscape gardener who was born in Northumberland. The dell is a secretive place, lined with rhododendrons, azaleas, camellias, and cedars of Lebanon. It is full of the sound of birds, hiding in the shrubbery. I watched a family there, regular visitors, their hands full of nuts and cake and similar tit-bits. The sparrows came to hand first then the blue tits and the great tits. The chaffinches ventured close followed by blackbirds, a jay, a magpie and finally a pheasant. I have never seen such tame birds. Soon there were nine species of birds around one child. A wren emerged briefly from cover and as quickly returned to the darker recesses of the rhododendrons. A robin tick-ticked its message and hopped round the perimeter of the assembled birds. The robin is by nature a woodland bird but it has adapted easily to the urban areas and nests throughout London except in the most densely built-up centre. It maintains itself in central parks with twenty pairs recorded, for example, in Hyde Park, achieving a higher density there than it does in the wild. It is the image of winter yet it suffers heavy losses in hard weather when the ground is frozen. Many a private back garden has its resident robin that seems to reappear year after year yet the annual mortality rate is something over 40 per cent and few birds live more than ten years.

At the northern end of Kew is the perfect antithesis to the wildness of the Queen's cottage grounds. In the walled garden behind the Queen's Palace, a rather ambitious description of the Dutch-styled house built in 1631, is a small formal space devoted to the plants that were contemporary with the house, an entirely seventeenth-century creation. Within the framework of low box hedges and clipped yew and bay are the herbs that spiced the dishes and cured the ills of early England. The labels not only give names but amusing quotations from early herbalists like Gerard and Parkinson. There is borage still in flower and some of the many species of viburnum. There is heart's ease and self-heal that makes all physicians unnecessary. There is mock privet for mouth ulcers and *Tulipa sylvestris* 'for them that have crick in the neck if drunk with red wine'. In one corner primroses are in bloom. There is never winter at Kew. Every season has its colour.

I could spend days in that small garden alone, with banks of *Sedum album* cladding the artificial mound raised as a viewpoint over the sunken garden and the pleached hornbeam arbour. Kew is not just a public pleasure ground, it is a place of science. Augusta, Dowager Princess of Wales started the botanical collection in a nine-acre site near the orangery in 1759 and some of the trees of that early stage still survive, like the Turkey oak and the oriental plane. It thrived under the influence of George III, the keen farmer who even made part of Richmond a farm for a while. Great botanists like Sir Joseph Banks and then Sir William Hooker gradually increased it to two hundred acres and established it firmly as a scientific institution, one of the finest collections in the world.

As the wind cuts more sharply from the river and the clouds gather, we can take refuge in the warm tropical dampness of the Palm House and see the great clumps of banana fruits rising above their fat foliage, the dark red male flowers in display. Coffee and rubber and great palms bring the smell of more distant countrysides. In the Fern House are plants that make bracken look very insignificant indeed. Pollution of the London atmosphere has moved the major tree collections into the Weald, at Bedgebury in Kent and Wakehurst in Surrey, but Kew still has enough to defy any idea that December is a dead month.

There are two ways of defeating winter. One is to introduce trees, shrubs, and flowers from other lands that will give greenery when the native flora is bare. Another is to create summer under a glass frame. Kew bears the palm but there are other lesser known Winter Gardens with small but valuable collections, one of the most notable being at Avery Hill near Eltham. It was created by Colonel North in the 1880s in the grounds of his new house, the focus of his eighty-six acre park. It has three rooms, the central temperate room, the tropical room and the cool house so you can move from camellias in flower to bunches of bananas in less than a minute. Amongst the giant ferns and palms and cacti are smaller wonders like the stag horn fern growing on the bark of a cork oak. The central dome of the Winter Garden is ninety feet high yet the Chinese palm beneath it, brought from Kew in 1962, looks uncomfortably close to the glass summit. Both the Winter Garden and the park with its fine collection of trees, eucalyptus as well as the native oak, are under the care of the Greater London Council which uses part of the grounds for its central nursery.

The drovers no longer bring their cattle on the hoof to Islington or Smithfield. In their place the enormous lorries gather in the early hours, their refrigerator plants breathing like latterday monsters, waiting to unload their cargoes of frozen carcases. Now the London markets are busier than ever with the produce of the British countryside and the delicacies from all parts of the world. While Covent Garden is only a ghost of its former self, Leadenhall, in the very heart of the City, cheek by jowl with the financial towers of Threadneedle Street and the Cheap, is as colourful as ever. This is still the chief game market, pheasants from the country estates, plump turkeys from Norfolk, wildfowl from the east coast marshes, the stall holders still busily plucking the feathers out.

For the sights and smells and noise that used to be Covent Garden we have to cross the City to the north-east beyond Bishopsgate to Spitalfields where Christchurch's obelisk and decorated, though faded, facade stands sentinel over the chaos of lorries and carts. Comice pears from Kent, golden delicious from France, oranges from Greece and Egypt, lettuce from the Netherlands, sweet grapes from Almeria, tomatoes from the Canaries. The City Corporation wool market and the knitwear shops, the oriental carpets and the soft furnishings keep the link with Spitalfield's history of the weaving trade and the Huguenots. In the flower market are the sprays of cypress, the sprigs of holly, the young spruce trees, the potted bay trees, the poinsettias with their crimson leaves, solanum with small berries golden as oranges, all ready to decorate the windowboxes of office and exchange, of church porch and City restaurant. I think of my father who started his day in 'the Garden' with rum and coffee at three in the morning as I wander round the stalls and try to see the mouth-watering produce with his experienced eye.

So London celebrates the culmination of the year with rural images. In Trafalgar Square the tall spruce tree from the Norwegian forests bears its unaccustomed fruit of the electrician's art. Under its artificial shade the ox and the ass and the lambs stand in enigmatic silence round a crib decked out in winter greenery. The crowds gather and sing and feed the pigeons and the black-headed gulls patrol the fountain's edge and join the clamour for food before taking a cold bathe. The starlings muster overhead in dark circling clouds, fresh from their suburban feeding grounds seeking the bright, warm centre at the dark hub of the year.

REFERENCES

THE RIVER

1 *Thames Survey*, 1625
2 W. H. Hudson, *Birds in London*, 1898, p.105, quoting Mr Tristram-Valentine
3 William Thomas Hill, *Octavia Hill*, Hutchinson, 1956, p.132

THE CITY

1 William Thomas Hill, *Octavia Hill*, Hutchinson, 1956, p.108
2 E. Moberley Bell, *Octavia Hill*, Constable, 1942, p.146
3 William Fitzstephen from John Stow's *Survey of London*, 1603, Everyman Edition, p.502
4 Royal Charter of the Gardeners' Company
5 William Fitzstephen from John Stow op.cit., p.502
6 S.E. Rasmussen, *London, the Unique City*, Cape, 1934, p.84

ROYAL PARKS

1 W.H. Hudson, *Birds in London*, 1898, p.118
2 Quoted by S.E. Rasmussen, *London, the Unique City*, Cape, 1934, p.92
3 C. Hart and C. Raymond, *British Trees in Colour*, Michael Joseph, 1973, Plate 4
4 Popular poem quoted by Dawn MacLeod, *The Gardener's London*, Duckworth, 1972, p.42

5 George Offer, quoted by C. Poulson, *Victoria Park*, Stepney Books, 1976, p.21

SPAS AND COMMONS

1 William Fitzstephen quoted in John Stow's *Survey of London*, 1603, Everyman Edition, p.502
2 From a broadsheet by John How (1684), quoted in W.J. Pinks, *History of Clerkenwell*, 1880
3 John Ruskin, *Praeterita*, 1899 (1949 edition, Hart Davis, p.37)
4 John Aubrey, *The Natural History and Antiquities of the County of Surrey*, 1719

GREENWOOD

1 John Stow's *Survey of London*, 1603, Everyman Edition, p.90
2 John Stow op. cit., p. 90
3 John Evelyn's *Diary*, 1641-1706
4 William Cobbett, *Rural Rides*, 1821
5 Lord Eversley, *Common, Forest and Footpath*, 1910, p.55
6 W.H. Hudson, *Birds in London*, 1898, p.167
7 Daniel Defoe, *A Tour Through the Whole Island of Great Britain*, 1724-6

DOWNLANDS

1 James Thorne, *Handbook to the Environs of London*, 1876
2 G.S. Maxwell, *Just Beyond London*, Methuen, 1927, p.106

EPPING FOREST

1 Daniel Defoe, *A Tour Through the Whole Island of Great Britain*, 1724-6
2 As quoted by E.N. Buxton, *Epping Forest*, Stanford, 1911, p.5
3 James Thorne, *Handbook to the Environs of London*, 1876

LONDON'S FARMS

1 John Norden, *Speculum Britainniae*, 1593

References

2 *Open Land and the Green Belt*, London Borough of Hillingdon Planning Department, 1973
3 William Pulteney, *Strawberry Hill*, eighteenth century

WATERWAYS

1 Michael Drayton, *Polyolbion*, 1612
2 William Thomas Hill, *Octavia Hill*, Hutchinson, 1956, p.164

DEER COUNTRY

1 John Evelyn's *Diary*, 1641-1706
2 *Hampton Court Palace*, HMSO, 1975

RESIDENT BIRDS

1 John Stow's *Survey of London*, Everyman Edition, p.93

ALL THAT IS GREEN

1 John Stow's *Survey of London*, 1603, Everyman Edition, p.89

Index

Abbey Woods, 72–3
Adam, Robert, 52
Agar, Ralph, 22, 26
Amelia, Princess, 115, 134
Apothecaries, Worshipful Society
    of, 11, 54
Aubrey, John, 55, 58
Ayrton, Michael, 29

Bacon, Sir Francis, 38
badgers, 86, 103, 136–7
Banks, Sir Joseph, 164
Barbican, 27–8
Barn Elms reservoir, 7
Battersea Fields, 9–10
Bayhurst Wood Country Park, 110
Bazalgette, Sir Joseph, 5
Beddington Park, 120–1
Bedfords Park, Havering, 129, 136
birds: in the City, 22–4; on
    commons, 50, 53; on the Downs,
    86–7; on estuaries, 4, 9, 12–14, 24;
    migrant, 117–20; in parks, 33–4,
    37, 41–3, 65, 135, 141; resident,
    143–55; near rivers and canals,
    122–4, 127–8
Bishopsgate, 25–6
blackbird, 148–9
Blackheath, 66–7
Bostall, 72
Brent river, 126; Park, 14
Brockwell Park, 102–3
Brown, Lancelot (Capability), 115,
    140, 163

Bushy Park, 139
Buxton, E.N., 96, 98
Byron, George Gordon, Lord, 112

Caesar's Well, 77–8
Caroline, Queen, 38–9
catalpa, 19
cattle, 91, 107, 109, 158
chalk, 78–81; see also Downs
Chambers, Sir William, 162
Charlton, 67
Chelsea, 8, 10–11
Childs, Sir Joshua, 94
Ching, river, 96–7
Chingford Plain, 97–8
Chislehurst, 61–2, 79
Chiswick House, 114–15
churchyards, 20–1, 25
City, 17–31
Cleary, W.E., 27
Cobbett, William, 71, 74, 107, 113
Colfe, Abraham, 55
Colne river, 119; Valley Park, 111,
    122
Coombe Wood, 88
Constable, John, 52, 53
coppices, 72
cormorants, 6–7
Coulsden, 82–4
Cray river, 73–4, 119, 127
Crayford Ness, 13
crows, 149
Crystal Palace, 54
Cudham, 81–2

daffodils, 17–18
Darwin, Charles, 80
deer, 65, 100, 129–41; fallow, 129, 136; red, 136
Defoe, Daniel, 72, 93
Devilsden Wood, 84–6
Dickens, Charles, 20
docks, 2–4; birds at, 3–4; farms, 3, 107
Downe, 80
Downs, the, 77–90
Dulwich, 55–7

elms, 82
Eltham, 70
Enfield Chase, 100
Epping Forest, 91–103
estuary, Thames, 12–14
Evelyn, John, 2, 31, 40, 55, 64, 67, 94, 100, 138, 139
Eversley, Lord, 51

Farleigh Green, 152–3
farms, 3, 105–16
fauna: on commons, 52–3; on the Downs, 86; in the Forest, 97, 103; in parks, 33, 42, 45, 65, 136–7
fish, 5, 35
Fitzstephen, William, 21–2, 25, 47–8, 74
flooding, 3, 8
flora: in the City, 17–18; on commons, 68; on the Downs, 85–6; Epping Forest, 97–8; in parks, 43, 52; by rivers and canals, 123–6
Forestry Commission, 128
Forty Hall, 100
foxes, 86, 136–7
Fulham, 6

Gainsborough, Earl of, 53
Gardeners, Worshipful Company of, 22, 36
Gerard, herbalist, 21, 52, 84, 163
Gilbert, Sir William, 113
gingko, 18–19
Goldsmith, Oliver, 30
Grand Union Canal, 122, 125
grasses, 89–90
Green Belt, 108
Green Park, 38

greens, 152–4
Greenwich Park, 36, 63–5
Grim's Dyke, 112–13
gulls, 7–8, 13–14, 38
Gunnersbury Park, 115

Hainault Forest, 97–100
Hall Place, 73–4
Ham Common, 138–9
Hampstead Heath, 51–4
Hampton Court, 140–1
Hanwell, 126
Happy Valley, 84–6, 121
Harefield, 109–11
Harrow Weald, 112–13
Harrys, Richard, 74
Hart, Cyril, 40
hawthorn, 149–52
heather, 131
Heathfield, 87–8
hedges, 149–52
Henry VIII, 2, 34–5, 63
herbs, 84–5; gardens, 10–11, 21, 54, 74, 163
herons, 6, 13, 42, 94
High Beech, 93; Conservation Centre, 98
High Elms, 82
Highams Park, 96
Highgate, 49–50
Hill, Octavia, 8–9, 20, 25, 51, 121
Holland Park, 41–2
Holwood Estate, 77–8
Hooker, Sir William, 164
hornbeam, 95–6, 100
Horniman's Museum, 57
Howard, Sir Ebenezer, 27, 78
Hudson, W.H., 7, 10, 33–4, 50, 72, 149, 162
Hunter, Robert, 51
Hyde Park, 33–4, 38–40

Inns of Court, 30–1

Jefferies, Richard, 56
Jones, Inigo, 30
Joyden's Wood, 128

Keats, John, 52, 53
Kensington, 38, 40–1
Kent, William, 114

Keston Common, 77, 133
Kew Gardens, 161–4

Lambeth Country Show, 102–3
lapwings, 144–5
Lea river, 100, 119, 123–5; Valley
    Regional Park, 123
Leyton Flats, 95
lichens, 41
lime trees, 40
Linnaeus, Carl, 66
London, George, 140

Mabey, Richard, 53
Mad Bess Wood, 110
marshes, 2–3, 12–14
Maxwell, Gordon, 80
May celebrations, 61–3, 67
Monken Hadley, 101
Moorgate, 26–7
Myddleton, Sir Hugh, 48

Nash, John, 38, 125
Norden, John, 31, 108
Northwood, 55

Osterley, 115

Parkinson, herbalist, 21, 163
parks, royal, 33–45
Parliament Hill Fields, 50–1
Paxton, Joseph, 54
Peckham Rye, 58
pelicans, 37
Pembroke Lodge, 137
Penge Common, 54–5
Pepys, Samuel, 25, 31, 154
Petts Wood, 62
pigeons, 22–3
Pitt, William, 77
plane trees, 11
Plumstead Common, 72
Pope, Alexander, 138
Postmen's Park, 29
Primrose Hill, 43
privet, 151–2
Pulteney, Sir William, 114

ravens, 24
Ravensbourne, river, 122
redstart, black, 28, 56

Regent's canal, 125
Regent's Park, 34, 42–3
Repton, Humphrey, 77
Richmond Park, 131, 134–7
rivers, lost, 103, 127
Rocque, John, 57, 152
Roding, river, 14, 94
Rookery, the, 58–9
rooks, 30
Roper, William, 71
Rotten Row, 35
Ruskin, John, 54, 88

St Dunstan's-in-the-East, 22
St James's Park, 34, 36–8
St Paul's, 17–19
Selsden Wood, 86
sewage, 5, 12
Sexby, J.J., 58
sheep, 53, 158
Shipton, Old Mother, 44
Shirley Hills, 87–8
Shooters Hill, 63, 68–70
Siddons, Sarah, 153
Smithfield, 29; Show, 157–9
snowdrops, 17
sparrows, 23, 148
spas, 55, 58; *see also* wells
spoonbills, 6
squirrels, 65, 136
Stanmore Common, 113
starlings, 145–7
Stow, John, 62–3, 155, 160
Streatham, 58
swans, 1–2
Syon Park, 115–16

Teddington, 139
Thames, 1–15; Conservancy, 5;
    docks, 2–4; estuary, 12–14;
    marshes, 2–3
Thomson, James, 137
Thorne, James, 102
Tojou, Jean, 140
Tower of London, 24–5
Tradescant, John, 11–12, 40
trees, 11, 19, 27, 159–61; on the
    Downs, 82, 84–5; Epping Forest,
    95–6, 98; in parks, 39–41, 45, 57,
    64, 138
Trent Park, 100–1

Turner, William, 115

Vauxhall Park, 8–9
Victoria Park, 44–5

Waltham Abbey, 100
Wandle, river, 120–1
Wanstead Flats, 94–5
Waterlow Park, 49
Watts, G.F., 29
Well Hall, 71
wells, 35, 47–8, 55, 58

Wells Park, 55
Westminster Abbey, 36
Westwood, 55
Wilberforce, William, 77
Willett, William, 62
Wilson, Sir Spencer Maryon, 51, 67
Wimbledon Common, 131–3
windmills, 132–3
Winter Garden, Avery Hill, 164
Wise, Henry, 140
Woolwich Common, 68

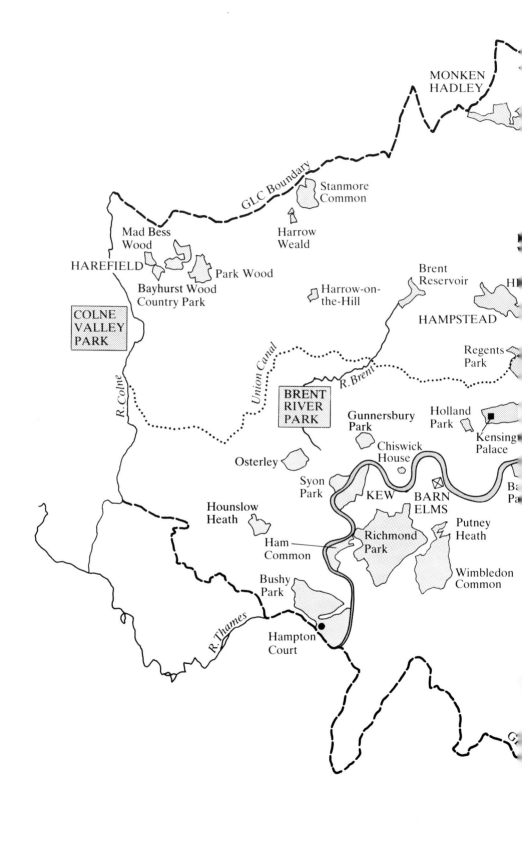

MONKEN
HADLEY

GLC Boundary

Stanmore
Common

Mad Bess
Wood

Harrow
Weald

HAREFIELD

Park Wood

Bayhurst Wood
Country Park

Harrow-on-
the-Hill

Brent
Reservoir

H

COLNE
VALLEY
PARK

HAMPSTEAD

Regents
Park

R.Colne

Union Canal

R.Brent

BRENT
RIVER
PARK

Gunnersbury
Park

Holland
Park

Kensing
Palace

Osterley

Chiswick
House

Syon
Park

KEW

BARN
ELMS

B
Pa

Hounslow
Heath

Richmond
Park

Putney
Heath

Ham
Common

Wimbledon
Common

Bushy
Park

R.Thames

Hampton
Court

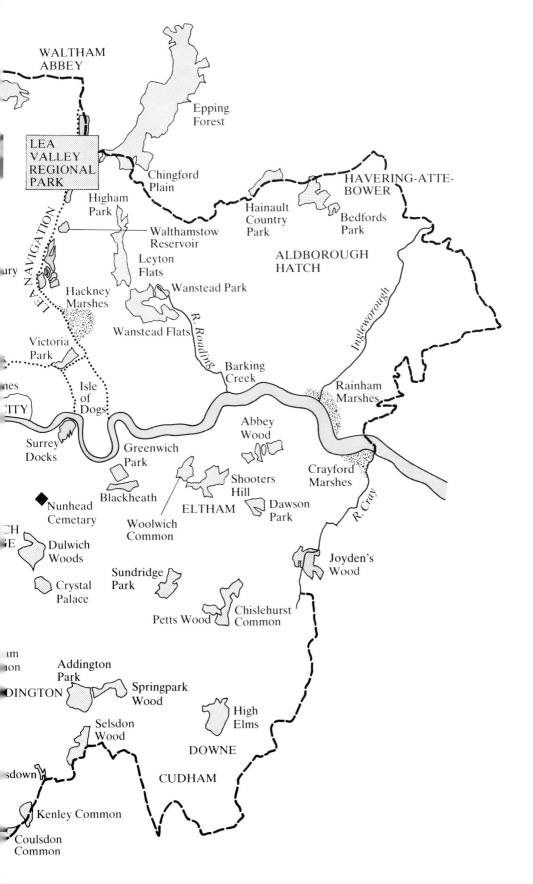